RESTLESS NATION

RESTLESS NATION

Accompanies the BBC Scotland television series

Alan Clements, Kenny Farquharson and Kirsty Wark

WARK CLEMENTS & CO. LTD

SCOTLAND *on* SUNDAY

MAINSTREAM
PUBLISHING

EDINBURGH AND LONDON

First published in Great Britain in 1996 by
MAINSTREAM PUBLISHING COMPANY (EDINBURGH) LTD
7 Albany Street
Edinburgh EH1 3UG

320.941

ISBN 1 85158 884 1

A catalogue record for this book is available from the British Library

Typeset in Goudy
Printed and bound in Great Britain by Butler and Tanner Ltd, Frome

1851   588   841   14.33

DEDICATION

For our parents

CONTENTS

Acknowledgments

This book grew out of the television series *Restless Nation*, first shown on BBC Scotland in 1991 and updated in 1996. We would like to thank Jim Hunter, then Head of Television, for backing the original idea, James Boyle, then acting Head of Television, for supporting the project and Colin Cameron, the current Head of Television, for seeing it through to completion.

The series would not have been possible without the encouragement of Ken Cargill, BBC Scotland's Editor of News and Current Affairs, the guidance of executive producer Val Atkinson and the creative input of director, Nicola Black.

From the beginning, *Scotland on Sunday* editor Brian Groom gave the book his full support. Colin Murray carried out invaluable research and writing. Thanks are due to Scotsman Publications for the use of its picture archive and to Liz Thomson and Susan Kemp for picture research. The library staff showed their usual patience.

Thanks also to Bill Campbell and John Beaton at Mainstream for bearing with us. John Curtice kindly read the copy at proof stage. Needless to say, any errors or omissions are ours alone.

In addition, the authors would like to thank the following for permission to use their images: The National Museum of Labour History, Fotopress, Scottish Labour Party, Stephen Mansfield, Scottish National Party, Outram Picture Archives (awaiting claim), Jim Turnbull (awaiting claim) and Stirling Press (awaiting claim). Special thanks to *SoS* photographers Adam Elder and Robert Perry.

Introduction

Restless Nation is a political portrait of Scotland since World War Two. The narrative focuses mainly on the long struggle for home rule that has given Scottish politics its vividness over the past half century. It is not the work of miniaturists, painting every detail with the help of a magnifying glass. Rather, we've tried to create a canvas which displays Scotland's political character: skittish, over emotional, capable of great gestures, prone to blame others and occasionally rather immature. Scotland is also blessed with, or damned by, an intensely complex set of loyalties and prejudices.

We each bring to this book a fierce love of Scotland, driven as much by family and cultural influences as by political journalism, our stock in trade. We also bring a sense of wonderment that, for such a small and essentially conservative nation, the past 50 years have seen such momentous shifts in its political direction. And yet the dominant feature on the canvas has remained unchanged. When you narrow your eyes, what you see is home rule, either an unsightly blemish or a mark of great distinction depending on the tint of your political spectacles. It perhaps unfairly overshadows other fine features.

Scotland is snagged on the home rule nail. We cannot seem to get away from it, or move on beyond it. We neither embrace it warmly nor shun it completely. For the population as a whole it may not be the first thing on their lips in the morning, but it touches them in some way. It might be displayed as an exaggerated chippiness at some perceived English sleight, or a debate about the possible erosion of an aspect of Scottish law, or embarrassment at some anti-English invective. The home rule issue is often dismissed as simply the confection of the chattering class, but it has been a mass movement at least twice since the war. Witness the fact that John Major has insisted that in this election, like the last one, defence of the Union will be his standard.

The nation we are discussing in this book is Scotland, but sometimes Britain as well, reflecting the continuing dual nationality of the Scots. In the 1990s Scottish loyalties are to Scotland and to Britain – sometimes only to Scotland, sometimes to both, but now rarely to Britain alone. It has taken a new Secretary of State to understand this fully and exploit it. Michael Forsyth has changed the tenor of the debate by playing the Scottish card so close to a general election, and so has ensured our sense of nationhood will be key to the campaign. Scotland is a nation. Britain is a state. We have felt this more keenly at sometimes more than others – in the 1970s rather than the 1950s. But perhaps for the first time, this assertion of nationhood is growing in England too. Rather than the more traditional appeasement of 'whingeing Scots', this past year has seen and heard a new distinctive fightback from English commentators. It intensified during the Euro 96 football competition, and is likely to be a factor in the general election campaign and beyond.

And what of the *Restless* of the title, from where does it stem? It reflects the ebb and flow of our desire for home rule. The pattern of Scottish politics is cyclical. The British establishment responds to demand for change by offering reform, usually delayed enough to miss the crest of the wave. And not even the most dyed-in-the-wool devolutionist would bet against this happening again. But the tidal charts show that with each wave of home rule the water moves further up the beach. Within a few months these waters will be tested again, and the outcome is by no means certain. When politicians talk about 'the will of the Scottish people' what do they mean? Objectively and actually, it does not exist, but the notion that sovereignty lies with the people, and not with parliament, is a peculiarly Scottish one which underpins the home rule debate.

In documenting the changes in the Scottish political landscape since 1945, there is also much that remains, depressingly, the same. We appear to be on a political loop of familiar questions, posed at regular interval but never satisfactorily answered. It was more than 20 years ago that Lord Kilbrandon recommended a reduction in the number of Westminster MPs under home rule and we are still discussing it. And then there's the resilient West Lothian question – now dismissed by Labour, but none the less potentially explosive. Yet we appear to be at a point when these intellectually driven questions come a poor second to the political and emotional consensus for a Scottish parliament.

Fifty years ago who could have predicted Scotland's politics in the 1990s? Labour is now the dominant force, and fully committed to home rule. But its on-off relationship with devolution – more than once overnight – has been a hallmark of Scottish politics. Talk of Labour trimming over tax raising powers for a Scottish parliament has a certain familiarity to it. And who could have foreseen the steady Tory decline in Scotland? In 1955 the Conservatives commanded a majority of the Scottish vote. No party has managed that since, and yet now they control not a single local authority in the country, can marshal just ten MPs, and cannot fill the Scottish Office without the aid of unelected peers. But political pundits would do well not to make the same mistake during this election as they did in 1992, of trumpeting a Tory wipeout. There is a small but unassailable Conservative support in Scotland.

In other European nations, conservative parties can safely wrap themselves in the national flag – but not here in Scotland. When John Major talks wistfully about a nation at ease with itself, and evokes images of cricket and warm beer, you can bet your bottom dollar it jars as much with Scottish Tories as with their political opponents. Conservatives in Scotland have in the past had their own home rule credentials, buried now, but perhaps not so deeply that they cannot be retrieved, if indeed there was ever a Scottish parliament. After all, Alec Douglas-Home only threw his weight behind the 'No' campaign at the last minute in 1979 because, he said, the Scotland Bill was not good enough. So now even Michael Forsyth realises that the status quo needs adjusting, a bit more sensitivity to Scottish pride, and where the opposition parties have misjudged Scottish Conservatism is in their assumption that unionism is somehow anti-Scottish, and unpatriotic. It has worked for almost three centuries and is a tough and resilient ideology. John Major and Michael Forsyth want to remodel it for the twenty first century and may well succeed.

The attack on the 'anti-Scottish' Tories has been led by the Scottish National Party, transformed from the 1950s when it was a tiny dot on the political map. Nationalists then would be astonished to see the party's new-found staying power and energy, regularly taking a quarter or more of the Scottish vote, and avowedly left-of-centre in its philosophy. Now largely made up of a fundamentalist membership, but led by the ultimate political pragmatist, Alex Salmond, the SNP is espousing a more gradualist approach, and the troops are staying in line.

And what of the keepers of the home rule flame? Having faced near extinction in the 1950s and 1960s, after being the great party of power, the Liberals, now the Liberal Democrats, had their glory times during the Lib-Lab pact, and brought a feverish air of expectation to the politics to the early 1980s. Now they are firmly positioned to take the whip hand in post-election negotiations if it's a close-run thing.

John Major has put the union at the heart of his politics. He does not underestimate the power of the Scottish vote. England got a government it didn't vote for in 1964 and again in 1974. It could happen again, and then what? For 17 years Scottish legislation has been passed at Westminster by dint of the Conservatives majority in England, but imagine a Labour government voting to abolish English grammar schools using Scottish Labour MPs.

Scotland could move in a different direction, if the will is truly there. But that remains the question. After the Referendum in 1979, the most memorable cartoon was Turnbull's image of a Scottish lion, a ball and chain on its hind leg, marked apathy, feart of the future. A national failure of nerve could happen again.

If this book works, it will be because it arouses the interest of people who've never been interested before or because it jogs the memory of many who may have become weary of the subject. For the committed, there have been many important academic books on the Scottish political condition, and this is certainly not one of those, but we hope they too might find this a sort of aide memoire. This book distills the thoughts of many writers and political scientists without the acknowledgement of footnotes, and adds our own observations and insights. This is intended as a popular book, one which demonstrates that this country of ours has a great capacity for political debate – often electrifying, more often frustrating, but never dull.

Restless Nation is a collaboration with *Scotland on Sunday* and it grew out of a television series first broadcast on BBC Scotland before the 1992 election, based around political interviews, and archive of key political events since 1945. Since that time several of our interviewees have died, Alick Buchanan Smith, John Smith, John Pollock, Judith Hart and Sir Robert Grieve. Their contribution not only to Scottish politics but to Scottish life was enormous.

Restless Nation now has another television episode bringing us up to this election. The series and this book go hand in glove. While television concentrates on the moving image, this is also a picture book which captures the most memorable moments in post-war politics by plundering *Scotland on Sunday's* extensive archive. It shows the nationalists' ability to make a splash, the powerful image of mass protest, the abiding predominance in Scottish politics of men in grey suits, but also the memorable inspirational figures and events.

Scotland's post-war story is one of a restless nation. We may soon know if that restlessness is to be stilled.

Alan Clements
Kenny Farquharson
Kirsty Wark
September 1996

CHAPTER ONE

British is Best

Labour Landslide

With the end of the war in Europe, party politics returned with a vengeance to Britain. Prime Minister Winston Churchill called an election, confident that the country would back the man who had steered Britain through its darkest days. He derided his Labour opponents as unfit for government, hopeless socialists who would require 'some sort of Gestapo' in order to rule. It was a dreadful political miscalculation.

When the election results poured in, a stunned Conservative Party found itself crushed. It was Labour's first-ever full general election victory, their overall majority an astonishing 146. Labour had never expected to beat Churchill and this result was beyond its wildest dreams.

Labour captured the mood of the time. Drawing on the spirit of democracy and common purpose engendered by the war years, Labour offered to rebuild Britain as a better place with collective answers to the old questions of health care, housing and employment. If planning could win the war, it could win the peace too.

'The Labour Party's great victory shows that the country is ready for a new policy to face new world conditions' declared a delighted Clement Attlee to the nation. When Labour MPs stood up in the House of Commons and sang *The Red Flag*, supporters across the country were euphoric. Everything they had struggled for throughout the 1930s and the war years seemed at last within their grasp. And Labour in Scotland sang along too, its 37 MPs flushed with the victory. But in their enthusiasm for the challenges of UK economic redistribution and and greater social justice, the party's historic commitment to Scottish home rule seemed like a distraction from the job in hand. It was sidelined. For Labour's Scottish MPs bigger – and British – was best.

The government went to work with a will. The 1942 Beveridge Report which proposed a national insurance stamp to protect Britons from poverty, was the inspiration of a slate of policies aimed at reconstruction and social reform. The task was formidable. The whole infrastructure of the country was in desperate need of repair and development. The appalling housing stock built in the inter-war years had to be torn down or upgraded. Before the war, hospitals had been run on charitable basis and their services were stretched to the limit. The Labour government's reforming zeal led it to legislate for almost every policy set out in their election manifesto *Let's Face The Future*. It nationalised the Bank of England and civil aviation (1946), the National Coal Board (1947), the British Electricity Authority and the Gas Council (1948). The creation of the National Health Service in 1948 was the jewel in its crown.

In the 1920s and 1930s Labour had maintained a commitment to Scottish self-government during its long years of opposition. In the 1945 election, home rule may have been out of sight, but it was not quite out of mind. While Labour's UK manifesto made no mention of devolution, a separate Scottish Council of the Labour Party manifesto made 'a Scottish parliament for Scottish Affairs' second priority after the defeat of Japan. But it was a commitment occasionally in the minds, but rarely in the hearts of Labour MPs and activists.

Tom Johnston, the inspiring wartime Labour Secretary of State for Scotland, set out the classic argument for devolution in a newsreel broadcast, declaring:

War is over: crowds celebrate the end of World War Two with an impromptu dance session at the Ross Bandstand in Edinburgh's Princes Street Gardens.

'All parties, classes and groupings sense the innate folly of administration 400 miles away.' But even to such a committed home ruler, the 1945 election seemed to guarantee Britain would be socialist and Scotland would be a full partner in the prosperity and improved standard of life that a Labour victory would bring. His successors, staunch unionists Joe Westwood and Arthur Woodburn, thought the demand for a Scottish parliament was reactionary, irrelevant and belonged in the past. The coming years would prove them very wrong.

Scottish Resistance

Despite Labour's coolness, the home rule torch burned brightly for a five-year period in the 1940s and 1950s largely fuelled by a non-party political organisation called the Scottish Convention. Though eventually extinguished, the Convention set a pattern for future outbreaks of nationalist unrest which would dominate Scottish politics for the next 50 years.

The Convention was the brainchild of the complex and charismatic John Mac-Cormick. MacCormick was a moderate nationalist who left the Scottish National Party (SNP) in 1942 when it elected Douglas Young, a fundamentalist nationalist and conscientious objector, as leader. MacCormick had a moderate approach to the war, compared to the fundamentalists who believed Westminster had no right to include Scotland in its declaration

Labour's general election campaign in 1945 captured the popular mood that it was time to build a new Britain. This famous election poster was inspired by Donald Zec, the Daily Mirror's wartime cartoonist.

17

of war. More importantly, MacCormick was also open to co-operation with other political parties, which was anathema to the hardliners. This tension between gradualists and fundamentalists would be continually replayed in the SNP's post-war story.

MacCormick resigned from the party, taking a considerable chunk of its support with him, and went on to form the Convention which in turn completely marginalised the SNP. Robert McIntyre had entered the history books as the first SNP MP when he won a by-election in Motherwell in April 1945, but he was rejected by the same voters in the general election just a few weeks later. This defeat marked the end of the Nationalists as a serious electoral force for nearly twenty years. James Halliday, the SNP Chairman in the late 1950s, recalls that the SNP was reduced to such a rump that all the delegates to the 1956 conference could stand together on their hotel steps in Bridge of Allan to have their photograph taken.

The Convention was much more optimistic. On 22 March 1947 it called together a 'National Assembly' with 600 delegates, drawn from all walks of life.

Labour's Tom Johnston served as Secretary of State for Scotland in the wartime coalition government, and espoused the home rule cause. Fifty years later, his style of government was cited as an influence by Tory successor Michael Forsyth.

The challenges facing the new Labour government were enormous, with a range of social problems requiring urgent attention. In the aftermath of war, some families lived for years in emergency housing, like this former army barracks in Lochinver.

In its ranks were eight MPs (five Unionist, two Labour and one Communist), four Scottish peers, town and district councillors, members of trades unions, representatives of co-operative societies and many more. It proudly declared:

'This assembly, representative of all shades of opinion, is convinced that a substantial majority of the Scottish people favours a large measure of self- government and therefore resolves to request that the government should forthwith introduce in parliament, a bill to give effect to the Scottish self-government proposals.'

The major parties stirred. Stung by the Convention's popularity the Labour government released a White Paper on Scottish Affairs in January 1948 which offered concessions to the home rulers – increased power for the Scottish Grand Committee to consider all Scottish bills at the second reading, a Scottish Economic Conference and an 'enquiry' into Scotland's financial relationship with England. It was administrative devolution to kill home rule sentiment.

Ironically the Scottish Unionists, as the Scottish Conservatives were then known, also saw an opportunity to get in on the act. Unionists attacked London-based socialist planning for riding roughshod over the the distinctive Scottish economy arguing, with some justice, that 'nationalisation meant de-nationalisation for Scotland'.

Miners working the seam at Newcraighall in 1949. Coal was one of a clutch of strategic industries nationalised by Labour in the late 1940s, including the Bank of England, civil aviation, gas and electricity.

To Labour fury, the Unionists withdrew their candidate in the Paisley by-election of December 1947, so that John MacCormick could have a free run as a 'National' candidate against socialist centralisation.

The Unionists also published *Scottish Control of Scottish Affairs,* a proposal for extra administrative devolution to Scotland, in particular for the nationalised industries. While ruling out consideration of a Scottish parliament and identifying the Union as a source of Scotland's strength, it also recognised Scotland as a nation in its own right.

Cynically the Unionists were hoping to attract Scottish patriots disillusioned by Labour's planning, which appeared to ignore every structural difference between Scotland and England. For the first time they had played the Scottish card. It was a card they would be tempted to play again.

Emboldened by the political stir it was creating, the Convention announced

Mothers take their babies to a new health centre at Sighthill. The creation of the National Health Service was, with the welfare state, the crowning achievement of Labour's 1945 administration.

its most ambitious project. On 29 October, 1949 it launched the Scottish Covenant, a petition which grandly declared:

'We, the people of Scotland who subscribe this engagement, declare our belief that reform in the constitution of our country is necessary to secure good government in accordance with our Scottish traditions and to promote the spiritual and economic welfare of our nation.

'We affirm that the desire for such reform is both deep and widespread through the whole community, transcending all political differences and sectional interests, and we undertake to continue in purpose for its achievement.

'With that end in view we solemnly enter into the Covenant whereby we pledge ourselves, in all loyalty to the Crown, and within the framework of the United Kingdom, to do everything in our power to secure for Scotland a Parliament with adequate legislative authority in Scottish affairs.'

John MacCormick's Scottish Covenant campaign drew a staggering response from the Scottish people, with more than two million signing the demand for home rule.

By the end of 1950, more than two million Scots had signed. It was a stunning achievement. Home rule stayed on the front pages. On Christmas morning 1950, the world awoke to headlines revealing that thieves had broken into Westminster Abbey and stolen the Stone of Destiny, the sandstone block on which Scottish kings had traditionally been crowned and which had been taken from Scotland by Edward I in 1296.

The search for the stone became a national obsession. To some this was an event capable of uniting a nation, a gesture to guide Scotland to freedom. To others, it represented all that was wrong with Scotland – a greater concern about symbols than reality. Leading Scottish Conventioner and author Nigel Tranter believes: 'The taking of the stone greatly excited the Scottish people. It created a

A Scottish Covenant Bond from the covenant campaign. It promised to pay the donor £500 plus interest when the 'Scottish government comes into being'.

Ian Hamilton, a leading light in the group of nationalists who repatriated the Stone of Destiny from Westminster Abbey to Scotland in the boot of a car. The audacity of the act set Scottish passions alight.

delirium almost. We are an odd lot, the Scots. We get terribly excited with our feet planted firmly in the clouds about things that are not desperately important, and the important things we sometimes let go of.'

But this student prank certainly galvanised the nation. Ian Hamilton, one of the students who took the stone, and now a QC, remembers being astonished. 'I thought there would just be a reaction in some political circles and that would be all but the whole hidden fervour of the Scottish people was there. It was as though we had pressed a button and brought a light on.'

James Halliday argues: 'It was the best single piece of publicity the Home Rule movement ever achieved. It captured the public imagination. It commanded total public sympathy. The public liked the symbolism. They enjoyed the insolence.' Eventually a stone – whether real or not remains open to debate – was returned to Westminister Abbey. But the Scots had demonstrated their distinctiveness as a nation once more.

Neither the publicity surrounding the Stone, nor the massive popularity of the Covenant could force genuine political reform. The Liberals, the only consistent parliamentary backers for home rule, were at their lowest ebb. The great reforming Liberal Party which dominated politics in the early twentieth century had been reduced to a group of squabbling factions by divisions over Irish home rule, free trade and how to combat the inexorable rise of the Labour Party. By the 1930s Labour had outstripped them. And worse was to follow.

In the 1950 election Liberal support collapsed. Across Britain, the Liberals lost 319 deposits and plummeted to a 9.1% share of the vote. They won just six seats with Jo Grimond their sole Scottish MP. When he took over the party leadership in 1956 he had a mountain to climb. Although the Liberal Party's commitment to Scottish home rule was wholehearted and genuine, it carried little political weight. The two major parties quickly realised that support for home rule was wide, but not particularly deep. So they successfully obstructed, delayed and waited for the economic recovery to kill the feeling. More importantly, Labour and the Conservatives realised the Convention was no electoral threat. Without that, it could be safely ignored. The Convention could do nothing with its success, and its frustrated and disheartened supporters started to drift away. For the post war Scottish resistance, gestures had to take the place of political victories.

The stone is recovered by the custodian of Arbroath Abbey. Tests ordered by the government satisfied ministers that despite at least one copy having been made, the 'real' stone had been returned. In 1996, 700 years after Edward I took the stone from Scone, the Tory government decided to return it to Scotland.

New Elizabethan Age

The early 1950s seemed to herald the dawning of a new glorious Elizabethan age. All across the UK, people marvelled at the wonders on display at the Festival of Britain in 1951, thrilled to the British conquest of Everest and enjoyed the end of rationing on sweets and chocolate.

But above all, a wave of British patriotism greeted the coronation of Queen Elizabeth in 1953. The pomp and circumstance of the ceremony seemed a recognition of past – and present – glories. Britain's sense of itself, its prosperity and its place in the world all seemed secure and something in which to take pride. The British side of the Scots' dual nationalism came to the fore.

The Queen's coronation in 1953 highlighted tensions in the Scots' dual nationality – their Scottishness and their Britishness. But the young monarch was always feted on royal visits, such as this one to Hamilton,

Nationalists fought a successful campaign to keep Elizabeth II off Scottish postboxes, such as this one at Inch. As far as Scots were concerned she was, of course, Elizabeth I.

The Conservative Party most effectively captured this mood, dominating British – and Scottish – politics throughout the 1950s. It won the 1951 election with a judicious mix of accepting Labour's social and economic reforms and promising to end post-war austerity.

The Conservatives saw through measures promised at the height of Covenant agitation, a report on Scotland's economic relationship with England and a Royal Commission on the government of Scotland. Privately Winston Churchill, restored to the Premiership, told Alec Douglas-Home to 'go up to Scotland and see if you can get rid of this embryo Scottish nationalist thing'. He succeeded.

The Cato report, the investigation into Scotland's financial relationship with England, was published in July 1952. In the first airing of the now familiar 'subsidy junkie' refrain, it concluded that Scotland did not pay its own way in the Union, drawing 12% of UK expenditure and contributing 10%.

Two years later, the Balfour Royal Commission on Scottish Affairs delivered its verdict. It was a body blow to home rulers. It acknowledged Scotland's difference, requested 'more sensitivity' from London government and criticised 'needless English thoughtlessness'. But it rejected a Scottish parliament and opposed further economic for the Scottish Office.

Winston Churchill finally resigned as Prime Minister at the age of 80 on 6 April 1955. His successor, Anthony Eden, led the party to its second consecutive general election victory just under six weeks later. In Scotland, the Conservatives took more than half of the total vote, a feat which has never been repeated by any party in any Scottish election since. The Conservatives seemed unassailable, and socialism and home rule discredited.

But it was not long until the Tories ran into trouble and, for the first time since the war, that trouble was deeper in Scotland than in England. The issue that eventually cost Eden his job and his health came not from the domestic political scene, but from further afield.

Tory Troubles

At the heart of Scotland's sense of Britishness was the British Empire. The Empire mattered enormously to the Scots and pride in its military prowess and feats of construction ran deep. As Tom Nairn argues, Scotland was not a neo-, near-, or any sort of English colony, but rather a junior, but enthusiastic partner in the highly successful enterprise of Anglo-Scots imperialism. The Scots need to face the truth. Whatever their feelings now, they enjoyed being part of the British state and Empire when it was at its height.

The 1956 Suez Crisis was the end of the British Empire. By then Britain's influence on world affairs was already waning. In 1947, Indian independence plucked the jewel from the crown of Empire and the financial drain of the Korean War was a warning that the maintenance of a global British presence was an unaffordable luxury. But delusions of power and grandeur remained.

When the Egyptian president Colonel Nasser nationalised the Suez Canal and demanded that Britain withdraw from its Egyptian base, Eden believed a plot to form a United Arabia under Communist influence was being hatched. Haunted by the memory of the failed appeasement of Hitler in the 1930s, Eden was determined to act decisively.

Britain, France and Israel struck in concert. But the campaign provoked a storm of international condemnation, particularly from the Americans, and the

Royal Marines occupy Port Said during the Suez crisis. Britain's ill-fated intervention in 1956 was a salutary lesson that Britain was finished as a world power.

allies were forced to abandon their positions, allowing UN troops to move in to police the border between Israel and Egypt.

Britain was humiliated. It had learned a bitter lesson: it was no longer a world power and could no longer act on the world stage without American backing. Britain, which took so much pride from resisting Nazi invasion and acting as a world leader just over a decade earlier, had to face reality. It was now just another medium-sized European nation with a collapsing Empire.

Elsewhere in Europe, nations which had been enemies in the war, learned the lesson of diminished power, and began to lay the foundations of unprecedented economic and industrial co-operation in the fledgling institutions of the Common Market. But not Britain. When the Treaty of Rome was signed in 1958, Britain was not at the table. In US Secretary of State Dean Acheson's famous phrase it 'had lost an Empire but had not found a role'. The same was true of Scotland.

The loss of Empire forced the Scots to focus again on what linked them to the other nations of the United Kingdom. Old loyalties began to crumble. Like the Empire, by the late 1950s, the Orange vote for the Conservatives in Scotland was in terminal decline.

Working-class Protestants had traditionally voted Unionist in Scotland. When the Scottish Unionists were formed from a merger of the Conservatives and Liberal Unionists in 1912, the Union they were defending was the one with Ulster, not the one with England.

Scotland and Northern Ireland were closely linked both religiously and socially, with the same sectarian divisions – albeit on a much lesser scale in Scotland. The Scottish plantation of Protestants in the seventeenth and eighteenth centuries provided the root from which the Protestant domination of Ulster society grew.

In the nineteenth and early twentieth centuries, the successive generations of Catholic Irish who flooded into Scotland in search of jobs, contributed to the complex social and political landscape in Scotland's industrial heartland. The poorer Catholics, leaving grim conditions of poverty and starvation behind them, would often work for less money than the increasingly unionised Protestants. The Protestant working classes reacted to preserve what they felt was rightfully theirs. Politically, they supported the Conservatives and Unionists as well as the independent Protestant parties which dominated many local councils in Scotland in the inter-war years.

By the end of the 1950s both ordinary Catholics and Protestants in Scotland found that their dreams of economic advancement were more in tune with a working-class Labour Party than a Unionist Party still dominated by landed and big business interests. The results for the Unionists were dramatic. In 1955 they held seven of the 15 Glasgow seats, including Govan and Central. Ten years later they controlled only two.

The Orange Order parades in Glasgow's George Square. Protestant support was instrumental in keeping the Conservative vote afloat in Scotland, contributing to the Tories' remarkable success in the 1955 election, when they took more than half the Scottish vote. Religious influence on voting then went into decline, but has never fully disappeared.

While the Orange vote was on the decline in the cities, it clung on in the mining villages and steel towns of the West of Scotland. It ceased to be a significant electoral force, though 40 years later the conduct of the Monklands by-election was a reminder that sectarianism retains a grip on Scottish society which still has the capacity to shock.

The Tories paid the electoral price for the decline of Scotland's traditional industries. During the years of reconstruction following the war, Scotland's heavy industries enjoyed boom times and there was virtually full employment. But by the late 1950s there was an altogether bleaker picture. Between 1954 and 1960 industrial production rose 9% in Scotland but 23% over the UK as a whole.

The increasing economic north-south divide had little immediate political effect. The home rule movement seemed completely crushed, and the two major parties were more unionist than ever.

*Jo Grimond, the dominant figure in post-war Liberal politics, is installed
as rector of Edinburgh University. Grimond brought the party back from
oblivion that threatened it in the early 1950s and paved
the way for a Scottish revival in the early 1960s.*

Hugh Gaitskell became Labour leader in December 1955. Within months of taking over he spelt out to the party's Scottish conference that devolution was an irrelevance. There was little resistance to the message. In a special conference in September 1958, the Labour Party in Scotland explicitly rejected home rule for the first time in its history.

Its concerns – and those of the trades unions – were to keep faith with national wage settlements and British planning. Willie Ross, who was to be the dominant figure in the Labour Party in Scotland for 20 years, argued 'Scotland's problems can best be solved by socialist planning on a UK scale.' As long as Scots perceived themselves as full partners in Britain's economic development, they would not demand more power over their own affairs.

The Conservative government was equally unconcerned about distinctive conditions in Scotland. It went into the 1959 election campaign full of confidence.

In the midst of an unprecedented consumer boom in England Prime Minister Harold Macmillan declared: 'Most of our people have never had it so good. Go round the country, go to the industrial towns, go to the farms, and you will see a state of prosperity such as we have never had in my lifetime – nor indeed ever in the history of this country.' The Conservative slogan said it all: 'Life is better with the Conservatives. Don't let Labour ruin it.'

But by 1958 the economic slowdown in Scotland had become a recession. Unemployment doubled to over 100,000, the worst since the hungry 1930s. Rallying calls of 'you've never had it so good' had a hollow ring north of the border. For the first time since the war a message shaped for English ears struck a discordant note in Scotland.

In the late 1950s, the message from the ruling Conservatives was that life had never been easier. Many people were experiencing a degree of prosperity, and consumer durables were marketed as lessening the load on the housewife. The British people were told: 'You've never had it so good.'

In the 1959 election the Conservatives were triumphantly returned with a majority of 100. It was an unprecedented victory – their third successive term in office with an increased majority every time.

But Labour could take heart from its showing in Scotland where it increased its share of the vote. It was the beginning of the end of the big Conservative party vote in Scotland – it lost five seats while Labour gained four. Never again would the Labour Party have fewer MPs in Scotland than the Conservatives. The Liberals stagnated and the SNP was still in the doldrums, attracting a tiny 0.5% of the vote.

But the most significant factor about the 1959 election was that Scotland had voted differently from England. It was a taste of things to come.

Harold Macmillan poured investment into Scotland, reckoning that a Conservative revival would be the consequence.

CHAPTER TWO

THE BEST LAID PLANS

A Plan For Scotland

The 1960s was a decade of great economic planning. Harold Macmillan's Conservative government unveiled grand blueprints for gigantic new industries in Scotland. Slums were cleared and their inhabitants rehoused in sprawling new estates on the fringes of cities and in sparkling new skyscrapers. The Conservatives were going to plan Scotland into prosperity and political peace.

The planning frenzy of the late 1950s and early 1960s suited the Conservatives in Scotland perfectly. Macmillan had been disturbed by the fact that, despite their overwhelming victory in England, Scotland had swung against the Tories. Now the Conservatives were seen to be doing something for Scotland. They were creating jobs. They were building houses. Surely, they reasoned, their political fortunes would be restored.

The intellectual basis for planning was the Toothill report on the Scottish economy, published in 1961. Sir John Toothill, the chairman of Ferranti, advocated planned growth, targeting Scotland's new industries and the New Towns. The Scottish Conservatives put aside their faith in the free market and willingly embraced this new philosophy. The government set up the Scottish Development Department in 1962 and quickly implemented its Central Scotland Plan. Scottish public sector expenditure and public sector employment quickly outstripped that of England.

The scale of the new policy was staggering For purely political reasons a vast new steel mill was sited at Ravenscraig. In May 1963, the Duke of Edinburgh opened the Rootes car plant in Linwood, the first car factory in Scotland for 30 years. It cost £23.5 million and aimed to produce 150,000 cars a year. The following December, the British Motor Corporation opened a huge truck plant in Bathgate.

Economically, the Scottish Conservatives were allowed to spend what they wanted. But the political bonus they expected proved elusive. Sir Teddy Taylor, then a Tory candidate in Glasgow, recalls the party's dismay: 'Everyone thought the answer to social deprivation was planning. We had lots of great factories set up. I think the most wonderful example of that

– the one that got everyone excited – was Ravenscraig. But one of the great surprises of this time was that we didn't get any political bonus for the Scottish Conservatives and Unionists. The tragedy was that the more money we spent, the less support we seemed to get.'

This was a problem the Conservatives could have done without. In spite of its massive majority, the Macmillan government was soon dogged by political misfortune.

In March 1962 the Liberals won a stunning by-election victory at Orpington. Two months later, a newspaper opinion poll put Liberal support at 30% compared with 29.9% for Labour and 29.2% for the Conservatives. Suddenly, the Conservatives' southern English suburbs seemed vulnerable. Macmillan panicked. In July he sacked six cabinet ministers in what became known as 'The Night of the Long Knives'. Liberal MP Jeremy Thorpe's searing quip summed up the public mood: 'Greater love hath no man than this, that he lays down his friends for his life.'

But this mass sacking failed to improve Conservative fortunes. Macmillan's 'big idea', his project to modernise Britain, was entry into the Common Market. In January 1963, after more than a year of negotiations, French President Charles de Gaulle snubbed Britain's approach, claiming it was not ready for full membership. Macmillan was humiliated.

Worse was to follow. In March 1963, John Profumo, the Minister for War, denied to the Commons any impropriety in his relationship with showgirl Christine Keeler, who was also having an affair with Captain Ivanov, a Russian intelligence officer. That lie was the start of the Profumo Affair, which dominated headlines all over the world and shocked the British establishment.

Floundering in a sea of political troubles, 'SuperMac' struggled to live up to his nickname. To add to his woes, he was faced by a rejuvenated Labour Party under its new young leader, Harold Wilson.

Wilson harried Macmillan mercilessly. But he also set out a new Labour stall. In 1963 he made a visionary speech declaring the need to manage a future full of change. 'That means mobilising scientific research in this country in producing a new technological revolution. Britain is going to be forged in the white heat of this revolution.' Under Labour, Wilson claimed the economy would grow as industry harnessed new technology and brought prosperity to all. But Wilson insisted that by planning that change workers would not lose their jobs as their workplaces became increasingly mechanised and their skills became redundant.

Macmillan's health gave way under the pressure and he resigned as Prime Minister in October 1963. The surprising choice as successor to 'emerge' from the smoke-filled rooms of Tory grandees was the affable and unflappable Scottish aristocrat, Lord Home, the first peer to become Prime Minister since

Christine Keeler's affair with John Profumo, the Minister for War, while she was also having an affair with a Russian intelligence officer, led to the minister's resignation, rocking Macmillan's already shaken government.

In the swinging 60s, the aristocratic Alec Douglas-Home was something of an anachronism. For the Tory party to pick him as its leader was regarded in some quarters as eccentric

the 3rd Marquis of Salisbury in 1902. To pave the way for his switch from the House of Lords to the Commons, he disclaimed his many titles including the Barony of Douglas and the Earldom of Home, becoming the almost plain, Sir Alec Douglas-Home. A young Tory candidate called George Younger – now Lord Younger – stood aside to let him be elected in the Kinross and West Perthshire by-election. As the candidate with the fewest enemies, Home's premiership avoided a civil war in the Tory party but still left it trailing in the polls.

In Britain's swinging 1960s this appointment seemed reactionary, even faintly absurd. Wilson milked it for all it was worth – the Tories were looking back and he was looking forward. Attacking 'this scion of an effete establishment', he bemoaned the fact that 'half a century of democratic advance . . . has ground to a halt with a 14th Earl'.

He titled Labour's 1964 general election manifesto *The New Britain* and campaigned against the '13 wasted years' of Tory rule. For the first time in a general election Wilson exploited the potential of television' using his comfort with the new technology to devastating effect in political debates.

Even so, the campaign was incredibly close. Given that the Conservatives were battling spiralling unemployment and a soaring balance of payments crisis, this reflected well on Sir Alec. After an awkward start, he even laid some blows himself, branding Wilson the 'slick salesman of synthetic science' and his manifesto 'a menu without prices'. Many voters enjoyed his old-fashioned decency and laughed when he parried Wilson by remarking: 'As far as the 14th Earl is concerned, I suppose Mr Wilson, when you come to think of it, is the 14th Mr Wilson'.

Lord Younger believes: 'He nearly brought the Conservatives back from a disastrous situation in 1963. I think he did a marvellous recovery job. The Conservatives had been in power for a long time so more people had things to gripe about. That's what happens after a long time in government.'

Sir Alec closed the gap, but it was not enough. The Conservatives' accumulated troubles proved too much. Labour squeaked in with a majority of six, its slender victory resting on a bumper return of 43 seats in Scotland. For the first time since the war the increasing north-south split in votes meant that England had a government for which it had not voted, a factor which went largely unremarked in those Unionist times.

The new steel mill at Ravenscraig was to become a symbol of Scotland's strength as a manufacturing nation – and then a symbol of its unrelenting decline. It was to be a pawn in political battles for 40 years.

The Moderator of the General Assembly of the Church of Scotland, James Stewart, visits the new Rootes car plant in Linwood just after its opening in 1963.

White Hot Heat

Scotland was addicted to the Conservatives' planning, but wanted more. The Labour Party was happy to oblige with a huge fix. Harold Wilson formed his cabinet and, in selecting his Scottish Secretary of State, made a decision that would affect the lives of ordinary Scots for a generation. It was the start of the Willie Ross era in Scotland.

Ross was a tough political operator. An elder in the Church of Scotland, he had a stern, schoolmasterly appearance and was a fierce and intimidating opponent in debate. He brooked no dissent in the Labour Party in Scotland. In truth, he faced little. Scottish Labour MPs mainly came from trades union and local government backgrounds. A parliamentary seat was a reward for long service, not an encouragement to enterprise and innovation. For most of the 1960s, Ross was

The appearance of Dounreay on the Caithness skyline was said to herald a brave new age of cheap, clean power. It was one of the presents for Scotland wrung from Harold Wilson by Willie Ross.

Scotland in the government, and the government in Scotland.

Ross's power in Scotland was given a boost when Chancellor George Brown unveiled his 'National Plan'. This replaced the Conservative idea of single 'growth points' to attract industry and investment with the more general concept of a broad Scottish Development Area. The Secretary of State for Scotland would decide the specifics.

Ross was zealous in pursuing Scotland's case with the Treasury. The pork barrel groaned as public expenditure rose 900% in Scotland between 1964 and 1973. A huge pit at Longannet opened, bringing 10,000 new jobs. Though the Conservatives condemned it as 'undiluted Marxism', Ross established the Highland and Islands Development Board in 1965. The Dounreay fast breeder reactor started in 1966, and the Invergordon smelter opened in 1968. The products of all this industry sped along new roads and across the great engineering marvels of the Forth Road Bridge and the Tay Road Bridge.

Scotland appeared to be on the brink of economic transformation. It

The nuclear submarine base at Faslane was a focus for anti-bomb protesters from the early 1960s on.

received a proportionately larger slice of Treasury funds than the rest of the UK and the gap between Scottish and English unemployment and investment narrowed. The political analyst, Christopher Harvie reckons Labour spent £641 million creating 105,000 jobs between 1966 and 1971, but 156,000 jobs were lost in agriculture and heavy industry. At the time however, it seemed Labour was delivering the goods, and the Scots were getting the socialism they desired.

The Scots rewarded Wilson with an electoral triumph in 1966. The new Conservative leader Edward Heath attacked Labour's planning with his '9–5–1' slogan (9% pay increases, 5% inflation and 1% growth) but the electorate was not impressed. All across the UK more people voted Labour than in 1964. In Scotland, the Conservatives lost three of their 24 seats to Labour. The party's triumph seemed complete. But Labour's leaders had disregarded a political shift happening at a grassroots level. Beneath the noses of Labour's leaders, Scottish sentiment was starting to stir.

The Natives Are Restless

By the early 1960s the first cracks started to appear in the monolithic two-party system in Scotland. A more educated, sophisticated and socially mobile electorate became less tribal in its party allegiances. Voters were prepared to flirt with new parties, and, once they had been unfaithful once, it was easy to be so again.

Also, the growing sense of Scottishness was fuelled by a sense of injustice at the UK government's handling of some sensitive issues. One which galvanised a generation of young Scots was nuclear weapons. A campaign of civil disobedience opposed the siting of Polaris nuclear submarines at US naval bases on the Clyde. If it came to nuclear war, the Scots knew they would be in the front line.

One of the campaigners, Labour MP Judith Hart, sums up the mood of the time. 'Polaris meant, here was Scotland already suffering economic injustice and social injustice and now it was to be the fall guy if there were to be a nuclear war. So, of course, Polaris produced a tremendous reaction and demonstration.'

In 1960, the Labour Party had adopted a policy of unilateral nuclear disarmament, leaving the leader, Hugh Gaitskell, outraged and promising 'fight, fight and fight again' against the policy. He succeeded in reversing unilateralism, leaving many Scottish Labour activists furious. At the Labour Party's Scottish conference in March 1961, a motion criticising the Holy Loch submarine base was kicked out on the grounds that it was not a Scottish issue.

But to many of the protesters, there was a definite Scottish dimension. It was as if a remote English government had decreed that Scotland was expendable. The perception that Scotland had been sold down the river to keep America happy toughened the campaign north of the border and gave it an edge lacking in England. Many campaigners who would normally have found a home in the Labour Party, such as Margo MacDonald and Isobel Lindsay, turned instead to the SNP. George Robertson, later Labour's shadow Scottish Secretary, was among the protesters, while his father, a policeman, was trying to keep order.

Another issue of concern to Scotland, and which fed into home rule sentiment, was Highland development. But here it was not the Nationalists who felt the benefit, but the Liberals.

In England, the spectacular by-election victory at Orpington in 1962 sent the Liberals on a, largely fruitless, search for suburban voters throughout the 1960s. But the Scottish Liberal Party was a very different animal with a proudly independent history. Throughout the post-war years, of all the mainstream parties, it consistently remained the most distinct from its English counterpart.

In the 1950s, the Scottish Liberal Party was, in Sir David Steel's words, merely 'the dying remnant of the once great party of government'. Reduced to a single MP and with percentage support in single figures, its very existence was in jeopardy. But charismatic leader Jo Grimond and Scottish Liberal chairman John Bannerman ensured it clung to life and brought a new generation into politics. The Scottish Liberal Party harvested youth dissatisfaction in Scotland's rural areas in the same way the SNP did in the central belt.

The first battleground was the Highlands. Bannerman, a Gaelic speaker and popular Scottish international rugby hero, railed against the lairds, with their semi-feudal control over the land contending, 'the Conservative political faith fitted their selfishness like a glove . . . the Highlanders continued to lick the hand that spurned them'.

Bannerman's attacks on the landlords were always linked to the Scottish Liberal priority of Scottish home rule: 'It was to wrest power from a couldn't-care-less Westminister government through the Liberal policy of home rule for Scottish domestic affairs that made me decide to stand as a Liberal at the hustings'. For Bannerman, the Scots needed to do more than sign petitions like the Covenant in the previous decade. They had to support political parties committed to home rule or, 'like slaves, our people will become fearful of attaining the freedom so long denied them'.

The Liberal 'Highland Strategy' paid off in a spectacular way in the 1964 election when the party wrested three seats from the Unionists. The Liberals appealed to a radical electorate tired of Conservative rule, but with little enthusiasm for central belt socialism. Even better was to follow.

Twenty-six-year-old David Steel stood as the Liberal candidate in the Roxburgh, Selkirk and Peebles by-election in 1965. The Conservative majority in the seat had already been trimmed at the general election, and, as Liberal leaders and activists newly enthused by the Highland breakthrough descended on the constituency, it crumbled. The Highland haul of seats was now matched with a Borders breakthrough. The Liberals were firmly entrenched in the politics of rural Scotland.

The SNP also gathered momentum. Partly inspired by the resistance to the nuclear bases on the Clyde, Scots began to look to the SNP. The party started to pick up votes in by-elections, 18.7% at Glasgow Bridgeton in 1961 and second place and 23.3% for William Wolfe against Tam Dalyell in West Lothian the following year. After these two performances, the SNP appointed their first full-time organiser and established constituency as well as branch organisations. The party claimed SNP membership rocketed from 2,000 to 100,000 between 1962 and 1968.

In the 1967 local elections, the SNP became real players on the political scene, taking over 200,000 votes and securing 69 seats on burgh and county councils. Then came the Hamilton by-election. On the face of it, the SNP candidate,

Winnie Ewing's by-election victory for the SNP at Hamilton in 1967 is regarded by many as the birth of modern Scottish Nationalism.

Glasgow solicitor Winnie Ewing, faced a daunting task. The previous Labour MP, Tom Fraser, who retired to take a plum job with the North of Scotland Hydro Board, had taken 71% of the vote at the previous election.

But the Labour government was struggling in the face of enormous problems. Following the vast spending on the National Plan, Labour struggled to balance income and expenditure. Chancellor James Callaghan attempted to cut public spending by imposing wage restrictions and increasing the duties on foreign imports. The dockers strike of 1966 seriously affected foreign trade and wrecked these attempts to stabilise Britain's worsening economic situation. As the value of the pound spiralled downwards, Wilson was forced to devalue and the National Plan collapsed. Wilson insisted the 'pound in your pocket' would be secure. The voters were not so sure.

SNP activists flooded Hamilton, their enthusiasm in sharp contrast to the

After the Hamilton victory, the Nationalists swept to success in local council elections, with veteran Robert McIntyre becoming provost of Stirling. He had been the SNP's first MP back in 1945. Growing SNP success jolted the Conservatives into considering Scottish home rule.

moribund local Labour parties of the central belt. The SNP said a litany of injustices faced Scotland at every turn. When the counting was over, Ewing was the new MP for Hamilton and the SNP once again had a voice in Britain's parliament. In an emotional speech, Ewing was exultant: 'Thanks to Hamilton for making history for Scotland. We are going to climb back onto that map again and get an independent voice at Westminister.' Her message was clear – stop the world, Scotland wants to get on. The SNP slogan became Free By '73, the first in a long line of over-ambitious Nationalist catchphrases.

The parallel rise of the SNP and the Liberals led them to consider partnership rather than rivalry. In one of the forgotten by-ways of Scottish politics both sides sought an electoral pact. SNP gradualists were close to Liberal federalism and many Liberals regarded the Nationalists as slightly errant and somewhat over-enthusiastic cousins. In 1964 and again in 1967 the two sides met. David Steel and Jo Grimond favoured a pact as did Willie Wolfe, later to become leader of the SNP.

But the talks foundered. Wolfe believes the Liberals were responsible as they insisted on the SNP adopting a federalist policy. Steel believes that after Hamilton the SNP was so elated it wanted to go it alone and its demand that a Scottish parliament should become the main priority of the UK Liberal Party was clearly untenable. Scotland's first cross-party electoral alliance fell at the first fence.

Nationalists were indeed cock-a-hoop. In the municipal elections in May 1968, the SNP produced its best result to that date. Despite a forbidding party political broadcast by Labour Secretary of State Willie Ross attacking separatism, the SNP took more than 30% of the vote and 100 seats. Dr Robert McIntrye, the SNP's first ever MP back in 1945, became the Provost of Stirling, while Glasgow was ruled by an SNP/Conservative coalition. Combined with the Hamilton result, this meant no Labour seat was safe. In the words of veteran nationalist Oliver Brown, 'a shiver ran along the Labour backbenches looking for a spine to run up'.

Unionism Restored

Hamilton was a huge shock to the Scottish political system. The Conservatives were the first to react. Pro-devolutionary Tory pressure groups sprung up. In 1967, the Thistle Group of federalists, including in their number future Tory ministers such as Michael Ancram and Peter Fraser, called for legislative as well as administrative devolution.

The Conservative leadership set up an informal working party to report to Ted Heath on the the need for action on what they called the 'national ques-

Edward Heath's Declaration of Perth at the Tories' Scottish conference in 1968 promised an elected assembly for Scotland, to the horror of many in the audience.

tion'. The Government of Scotland Policy Group, under chairman of Scottish and Newcastle Breweries and Tory grandee Lord William Younger, secretly briefed the Tory leader and tried to provide him with a rudder as he sailed into uncharted devolution waters. The group asked him to consider going beyond purely administrative devolution and to give the Scots some real power over their own affairs. The result was a huge political storm.

When he addressed the Scots Tories gathered in Perth in 1968, Heath was in confident mood. He declared resoundingly: 'We are pledged to give the people of Scotland genuine participation in the making of decisions that affect them and to do so within the historic unity of the United Kingdom.' Arguing a Royal Commission would be 'too large, slow and cumbersome', Heath proposed setting up a constitutional committee to look at devolution then concluded: 'We would propose to the constitutional committee the creation of an elected Scottish assembly to sit in Scotland'.

Labour Cabinet minister Barbara Castle visits Linwood.
She eschewed the red carpet laid out for her when a man called out:
'Come in the workers' entrance, Barbara!'

George Younger, one of the Conservatives then urging Heath to make the announcement, will never forget the moment. 'When he spoke the actual sentence there was a sort of shock wave around the hall. Half the people had never expected anything like this. Of course, some of them were very pleased. Others were pretty horrified. What we had done by getting him to make this declaration was to get a place for the Conservatives at the devolution debate. And we were able to demonstrate what could be done within the UK.'

Others had grave doubts, Bob Kernohan, then the new full-time Scottish Conservative and Unionist Party director, is candid about Conservative motives: 'I think the atmosphere following the Hamilton by-election – when of course we never knew when another by-election might be sprung on us and things would go from bad to worse – the atmosphere certainly caused the haste with which the

Declaration of Perth was produced. The Conservative Party was alarmed almost to the point of panic and was certainly alarmed into doing things more hastily than would have been wise.'

Heath immediately set up the promised constitutional committee headed by Lord Home. In March 1970, it published *Scotland's Government*. This report proposed a directly elected Scottish Convention, 125-strong, to meet 40 times a year. Essentially, it would take on the work of the Scottish Grand and Standing Committees, framing legislation, co-ordinating Scottish views and questioning ministers. But the UK parliament would always have the final say and third readings of bills would remain at Westminister. Heath accepted these recommendations and, however weak the Home proposals, the Scottish Conservatives entered the 1970 election as a devolutionary party.

The Labour Party acted equally decisively to deal with devolutionary demands. But it preferred the stick to the carrot. At the 1968 Scottish Labour conference, Willie Ross launched a vehement attack on nationalism. Urged on by his fervour, the party threw out a resolution by the Hillhead constituency Labour Party proposing support for a Scottish parliament. The Scottish Labour establishment did not want to be seen to be appeasing nationalism. There would be no surrender to separatism. When the Scottish Trades Union Congress came out in favour of devolution, Ross tore into them, warning them against taking refuge in the 'quicksands of nationalism'. He derided the SNP as 'Tartan Tories' and branded them the 'Scots Narks'.

Ross was an enigma. In private he was an ardent nationalist – with a small 'n' – but in public he vigorously rejected home rule. He argued the best way forward – the way that worked – was for him to fight Scotland's case in the Cabinet. His philosophy could be summed up as, 'Who needs devolution when you have got me?'

Jim Sillars, then a young Labour candidate, remains puzzled by Ross: 'Ross in private was one of the most Scottish nationalistic figures I've ever met. He could say things at Burns suppers or in private – anti-English in their make-up – that I would never dream of saying. But he was simultaneously quite adamant that Scotland should remain an integral part of a unitary state with England. I could never quite work out this paradox in the personality of Willie Ross.'

John Pollock, who knew Ross well and who chaired the Labour Party in Scotland in 1959 and 1971, agreed. 'Willie Ross was strangely enough almost the archetypal Scot. He would be seen outside of Scotland as one of the strongest nationalists there has ever been. If Willie Ross had chosen to lead the nationalists rather than to fight them we might be in a quite different position today.'

But he chose to fight them, and fight them hard. Ross argued in Cabinet that Hamilton was a freak result, the product of a protest vote that the party simply had to endure until it went away.

Harold Wilson, as ever, wanted to keep his options open. He feared the rise of the Liberals and the SNP indicated Labour had got it wrong on home rule. He appointed the pro-reform Judith Hart to oversee a strategy for devolution. But, as the nationalist threat receded, she was quietly dropped, and Ross reigned supreme.

It seemed to work. Part of the reason it did was the inexperience of the nationalists. The SNP had grown too fast and lacked any ideological anchor. Its electoral triumph had overwhelmed the party organisation. Willie Wolfe acknowledged that many of the new SNP councillors knew little about what they were expected to do. Some, surprised by their success, even resigned immediately.

The ideological question was even more difficult. With whom should the SNP councillors vote? Conservative or Labour? And, as the party grew, the old split between fundamentalists and gradualists re-emerged. In 1969, Wolfe won a bruising leadership battle with Michael Grieve, son of Christopher Grieve, better known as the poet Hugh MacDiarmid. Grieve wanted an all-out attack on the Labour Party while Wolfe counselled: 'you don't attack those you need to win over'. The bandwagon started to shake.

In the 1970 South Ayrshire by-election, the Labour Party candidate was the staunch unionist Jim Sillars. The young Sillars, furious at Winnie Ewing's attack on the integrity and patriotism of Labour Party members, had written *Don't Butcher Scotland's Future* in 1968, an assault on the SNP and devolution. In the by-election, he went for nationalism's Achilles heel. In this solid working-class constituency the SNP refused to say whether it was a socialist party for fear of losing votes elsewhere. It was a costly strategy. Labour triumphed. The SNP bandwagon was derailed.

In the general election later that year, Ted Heath led the Conservatives to a surprise victory which included the recapture of two Liberal seats in the Highlands. The cosy two-party consensus seemed totally restored, but it was only a lull before the stormy 1970s.

CHAPTER THREE

PLAYING THE SCOTTISH CARD

The Popular Challenge

In the 1970s, Scotland's constitutional restlessness came to a head. The home rule 'Scottish Question' dominated political life both north and south of the border. Each of the political parties manoeuvred relentlessly, attempting to play the right Scottish card.

Yet it all started quietly. A 4.8% swing to the Conservatives gave Ted Heath a surprise victory in the 1970 general election and a comfortable majority of 30 in the new House of Commons. But Gordon Campbell became the first Secretary of State for Scotland since the war to represent a government that had neither a majority of seats, nor a majority of votes in Scotland.

Campbell's first task was to deal with Lord Home's report with its proposal for a devolved Scottish Convention. The SNP's relatively poor performance at the general election, where it won only 11.4% of the vote, lost Hamilton and gained just the Western Isles, offered Campbell an opportunity to fudge the issue.

At the Scottish Conservative conference in May 1971, he demonstrated just how little the Tories were going to do about devolution – the very policy that Heath had made a key plank in the Conservatives' manifesto only a year earlier. Instead of establishing the Convention, Campbell announced it would be one of the options in a 'possible' Green Paper. Just three years after the Declaration of Perth, in the words of academic Jim Mitchell, 'the Tory commitment to a Convention had been reduced to an uncertain intention to include it in a discussion paper amongst other possibilities at some unspecified future date'. Heath was driven by a desire to join the growing union of European nations, not to tamper with the union between Scotland and England. For the Scottish Conservatives, devolution was dead.

However, it was not Heath's dismissive attitude to home rule which made the most impact in Scotland, but rather his approach to economics. The Conservative Party had embraced the principles of the welfare state and economic planning in the 1950s and it struggled to define what set it apart from Labour. In Scotland Conservative spending plans could always be outbid by

Labour ones. During the years of opposition in the late 1960s, Heath had become convinced that Britain was sick and in need of drastic surgery.

In January 1970, five months before the general election, the shadow Cabinet met at Selsdon Park and adopted a dramatic new policy. The cosy consensus was to cease. The new Conservative call was for more competition, tax cuts, a more discriminating approach to welfare and a crushing of union power. Heath insisted people should keep more of their own money and learn to stand on their own two feet. And so too with business. If industries were terminally ill, they should be allowed to die. No more would government aid be used to prop up 'lame ducks'.

When he won power, Heath went to work with a will. He slashed government grants and passed a radical Industrial Relations Act which curbed trade union rights. The unions reacted furiously, making 1970 the worst year for strikes since the General Strike of 1926. Unemployment in Scotland leapt 43% in the first year of the new Heath government. The medicine was unpalatable, but Heath was determined to stick to his prescription. Then came UCS. In June 1971, Upper Clyde Shipbuilders announced it was going into receivership. The future looked grim for the 8,500 employees. But they were determined not to lengthen Scotland's dole queues. Led by two youthful and charismatic Communist shop stewards, Jimmy Reid and Jimmy Airlie, the workers locked themselves into the yard and kept working.

The emotional significance of the Clydeside yards to Scotland's sense of itself was fundamental. This meant the UCS work-in rapidly became the symbol of Scottish resistance to the changing industrial order, particularly the decline of the country's heavy industry. Reid in particular knew how to work the media and harness public sympathy. The work-in was a brilliant propaganda coup, a clever reversal of the stereotype of the work-shy and strike-prone labour force. In a mass meeting, Reid stressed to the workers the importance of image: 'The shop stewards representing the workers are in control of this yard. And there will be no hooliganism, there will be no vandalism, there will be no bevvying. The eyes of the world are watching us and it is our responsibility to conduct ourselves responsibly, and with dignity and with maturity.'

The thought of losing one of Glasgow's great shipyards seemed to many Scots symbolic of the callous values of a government for which they had not voted. Money and offers of support poured into the campaign. Reid recalls how the struggle blossomed. 'The UCS campaign started off as a fight for the yards. Then it developed into a fight for the right to work. Then it developed into a fight for the Scottish economy, and the needs of the Scottish people and the need for the Scottish people to have some control over their own destiny. And I think after a few months there was a growing realisation that this one, this one could be won.'

Jimmy Reid found fame as one of the leading shop stewards in the work-in at Upper Clyde Shipbuilders (UCS), calling for dignity, solidarity and 'no bevvying'.

UCS workers vote during the work-in, which lasted 16 months and resulted in a climb-down by the Tory government

He was right. When Rolls-Royce's aero division hit severe financial difficulties just a month after the work-in began the government nationalised it to save it from closure. Gordon Campbell was determined UCS should not be treated differently from Rolls-Royce.

On 21 June 1972, the STUC met Heath to discuss the UCS crisis. Two days later, 80,000 people marched to a rally on Glasow Green in support of the yard. The government caved in. After a 16-month work-in, UCS was reprieved and industrial development grants restored. Scotland had forced a change in Conservative policy and the phrase 'U-turn' entered the political dictionary. Protest could work, and it was contagious.

Between 1972 and 1974, Heath's government struggled against unparalleled industrial and economic problems. The Industrial Relations Act was opposed by the unions at every turn, particularly when the jailing of five Liverpool dockers created instant martyrs.

In Scotland, 25 local authorities defied a Housing Act requiring them to raise rents. Over and over, the Scots mantra was that this government had no mandate for its actions.

Then the oil crisis hit. The Yom Kippur War between the Israelis and the Arabs in 1973 made the Arabs realise how potent oil could be as an economic weapon. Their limiting of production quadrupled prices, which led to huge balance of payments problems for the British government.

Blow after blow struck the Tories. Unemployment soared to one million for the first time since the war. Inflation leapt to 18% by November 1973, leading to the Conservatives introducing a restrictive, wage policy to bring it under control.

But Heath's biggest struggle was with the miners. They refused point blank to accept the Conservatives' pay policy. On 12 November, 1973, the miners called an overtime ban. The next day Heath responded by declaring a state of emergency. By mid-December, power cuts led to most Britons working a three-day week.

It took until early 1974 for Heath to run out of patience. When the miners called an all-out strike for 9 February, Heath took the country to the polls demanding to know 'Who Governs Britain?'

The electorate was not sure. The Conservatives won more of the popular vote than Labour. Labour won more seats but failed to secure an overall majority. Most strikingly, many voters called a plague on both their houses and turned to third parties. Six millon people voted Liberal – 19% of the UK electorate. But the most spectacular performer of all was the SNP.

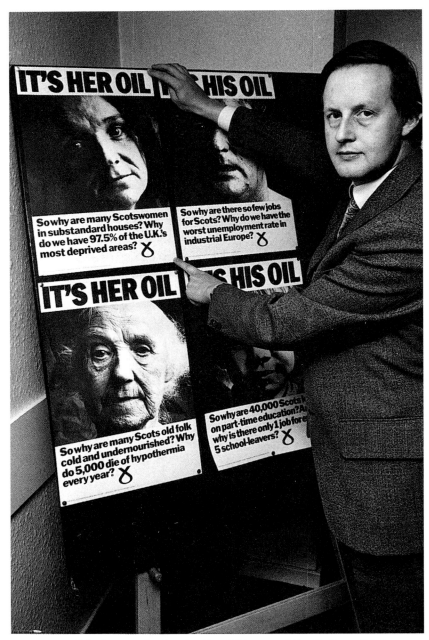

Astute political campaigning by the SNP turned North Sea oil into one of the key issues in Scotland during the 1970s. Gordon Wilson later became party leader.

Nationalism on the March

The UCS crisis had united Scottish sentiment against the Conservatives, but it was the discovery of oil in the North Sea which transformed nationalism into a credible political creed. Almost overnight Scotland's economic prospects changed from the steady and inevitable decline of heavy industry to the luxury of potential oil-state opulence.

In 1971, not long after the first major BP oil strikes in the Forties Field, veteran SNP activist Robert McIntyre ran Labour's Harry Ewing close in a by-election in Falkirk and Stirling. In 1972 the SNP started to develop its oil campaign. Against a backdrop of spiralling unemployment and industrial unrest, it began pushing the seductive economic argument that if Scotland could opt-out of the dreary present and uncertain future of the failing British state, then riches awaited. Posters and stickers all over Scotland baldly declared, 'It's Scotland's Oil' and 'Scotland's Oil – To London With Love'. The campaign's second wave offered a stark choice: 'Rich Scot or Poor Briton?' The quadrupling of oil prices may have been a nightmare for Britain's balance of payments, but it underscored how well-off Scotland could be.

In 1973, the SNP snapped at Labour's heels in the Dundee East by-election before Margo MacDonald, the 'blonde bombshell' beloved of the tabloids, won the Govan by-election that November in spectacular fashion.

She has no doubts why she won: 'the SNP's oil campaign at that time was absolutely vital because the argument had always been in Scotland: "oh, it would be lovely to have our own parliament, but we couldn't do it, couldn't afford it, who would pay for it?" The oil campaign put paid to that argument.'

The February 1974 general election three months later was a triumph for the SNP. It took 22% of the vote and seven seats, including the scalp of Scottish Secretary Gordon Campbell. The SNP drew voters from all parts of the electorate, but particularly the young and socially mobile. The poorest, and Catholics were the most resistant. Professor Bill Miller's research showed that, compared with the 1970 general election, the SNP won 40% of the 1970 Liberal vote, 40% of those who abstained and 44% of voters who had been too young to vote in 1970.

The Labour Party was in a poor position to defend itself. Helen Liddell, Scottish secretary of the party between 1977 and 1988, remembers the problem all too well.

'Throughout the 1960s and early 1970s there had been an atmosphere of decay about the Labour Party. There had been corruption scandals. There was also this general feeling that Labour could put up a monkey, and that monkey would be elected. And, as a result, the electorate began to get browned off. So

Labour's Robin Cook on the stump in Edinburgh in February 1974. He was sceptical about devolution and would be a leading light in the Labour Says No campaign in 1979.

there was a beginning of an upswing of the Scottish Nationalists. They seemed vibrant. They had a strong case. They had some very charismatic leaders. And it was very different from the rather tacky-looking Labour Party and the élite and distant Conservative Party.'

The next six months were traumatic ones for Labour in Scotland, with the party completely changing its position on home rule. The rise of the SNP was throwing its domination of Scotland into doubt. This could not be tolerated.

In 1968 the Labour government had set up a Royal Commission under Lord Kilbrandon to investigate home rule. It finally reported in October 1973 in favour of legislative devolution which it defined as 'the delegation of central government powers without the relinquishment of sovereignty', but said this would mean abolition of the office of Scottish Secretary and a reduction of Scottish MPs from 72 to 57. Labour rejected its conclusions and had gone into the February election opposed to any form of home rule.

Within a week of the election, Labour had changed its mind. Its Scottish executive issued a statement: 'There is a real need to ensure that decisions affecting Scotland are taken in Scotland wherever possible . . . we believe this might best be done by the setting up of an elected Scottish Assembly . . . but there can be no question of reducing the number of Scottish MPs or abolishing the position of Secretary of State.' Despite the obvious caution, the lid had been lifted on a tightly canned debate within the Labour movement. It could not be replaced.

Harold Wilson's minority government initially only promised to bring forward proposals for discussion, but, when pressed by Winnie Ewing during the debate on the Queen's Speech, Wilson promised a White Paper and a Bill. Within three months Labour published a White Paper, *Devolution In The UK – Some Alternatives For Discussion*, which set out five options for change.

Many in the Labour Party in Scotland, however, still regarded any flirtation with devolution as fatal appeasement of the Nationalist enemy. On 22 June 1974, just 11 of the 29 members of the Scottish executive of the Labour Party gathered to consider the White Paper – the rest were watching Scotland play Yugoslavia in the World Cup. By a vote of 6 to 5, the executive rejected all five options.

The British Labour leadership was furious. Roy Jenkins, then Home Secretary, is candid about the Cabinet's thinking throughout this time: 'The fundamental trouble was that the Labour Party leadership, I think this was true of Wilson, I think it was true of Callaghan, I think it was to some substantial extent true of Willie Ross, saw the need for some devolution to avoid losing by-elections to the Nationalists and not to produce a good constitutional settlement for Scotland and the UK. Any question of separation would be very damaging for the Labour Party because, while it might give Labour a very powerful position in Scotland, if you did not have Scottish members of parliament playing their full

The SNP used humour in its campaining to better effect than any party had before, as in this cartoon of Heath and Wilson.

Harold Wilson in Leith during the October 1974 general election.

part in Westminster then the Labour Party could pretty much say goodbye to any hope of a majority ever in the UK.'

Labour's national executive committee ordered a special conference to reverse the decision. The Scottish party met at the Co-operative Halls in Dalintober Street in Glasgow in August 1974. After a bad-tempered and bitter debate, the leadership used the union block vote to push through an agreement on the principle of devolution. It was an historic change, and Labour has remained – at least officially – a home rule party ever since.

Wilson decided to go to the country in October 1974 to try to get a working majority. Going into the election, Labour made devolution the central plank of their platform. Opting out of the UK party political broadcast, the Labour Party in Scotland produced one of their own, devoted entirely to devolution, in which the devolved assembly was repeatedly called a parliament, complete with powers of taxation and revenue.

The SNP sent a 'football team' of 11 MPs to Westminster in the autumn of 1974.
Left to right: Douglas Crawford, George Reid, Gordon Wilson, Douglas Henderson,
Winnie Ewing, Donald Stewart, Margaret Bain (later Ewing), Hamish Watt, Iain
MacCormick, Andrew Welsh and George Thompson.

Oil dominated the campaign. The SNP demanded all the revenue for Scotland. The Liberals thought Scotland should get half. The Conservatives wanted to establish a Scottish Development Fund secured by oil revenues, but Labour still maintained that the black gold was a British resource.

After a bitter campaign, Labour marginally improved its position, and Wilson was returned with a majority of just three. In Scotland, the SNP's share of the vote leapt to over 30%, and it won 11 seats. The SNP's 'football team' was on its way to Westminster. Although the SNP gains were at the expense of the Conservatives, Labour was alarmed.

Winnie Ewing remembers why: 'In the second election of 1974 we really beat the credibility gap as we got 11 out of the 72. But, as Michael Foot said to me: "it is not the 11 of you that terrify me so much, Winnie, it is the 42 seconds." You see, we were second in 42 seats plus the 11.' This performance ensured home rule would stay top of the UK agenda.

The Unionist Response

After the October 1974 general election, the struggle for Scottish self-determination switched stage decisively from Scotland to Westminster. For the next four years, devolution dominated parliamentary life and became increasingly bound up in the Labour government's desperate struggle for survival.

But if Labour was split and hesitant on home rule, so were the Tories. In the early 1970s the Conservatives had three policies in as many years, favouring at successive annual conferences first an indirect assembly, then no assembly, then a directly elected one.

A few days after the October general election, Alick Buchanan-Smith, the new Shadow Secretary of State for Scotland, tried to sort out the mess. Flanked by George Younger and Teddy Taylor, he held a press conference, and called for a directly elected assembly.

Six months later, Margaret Thatcher replaced two-time loser Ted Heath as Tory leader. She seemed to embrace devolution eagerly. Addressing a rally in Glasgow City Hall, she pledged that an 'assembly must be a top priority to ensure more decisions are taken in Scotland for Scotsmen'. Devolution seemed to have cross-party support, but the devil was in the detail.

In November 1975 Labour published *Our Changing Democracy* which proposed a 142-seat assembly, funded by an annual block grant, which would have control over most Scottish Office functions. It would have no control over the newly created Scottish Development Agency (SDA), and in areas of conflict between the assembly and Westminster, the Secretary of State for Scotland would decide the limit of the assembly's powers.

The weakness of the proposed bill was too much for some. After much soul-searching, Jim Sillars left Labour and set up the breakaway Scottish Labour Party (SLP) in January 1976, taking with him another MP, John Robertson, and Alex Neil, then a research officer with the Labour Party. The SLP demanded a parliament with real economic teeth.

The SLP struggled to find a niche in the political system north of the border, where it was squeezed between the increasingly pro-devolutionary Labour Party and the popularity of the SNP. It attracted very little grassroots support and became mostly the preserve of the intellectual left. It finally disbanded after the 1979 election in a welter of factional in-fighting and allegations of infiltration by fringe Marxist groups.

Opinion remains divided on the significance of the SLP. Many in the current Labour leadership see it as an ideological adventure which robbed the Labour Party of Sillars, its most eloquent exponent of home rule. Sillars himself maintains that the SLP exerted considerable influence on Scottish political

Willie Ross, as Wilson's Secretary of State for Scotland, was an enigma.
A dogged fighter for Scotland in Cabinet, he posed the question:
Why do you want home rule when you have me? He resigned as
Secretary of State in 1976 when Harold Wilson left Number 10.

thinking, and was a precursor to the SNP's later dialogue with the Scottish left.

In March 1976, Harold Wilson stunned the political world by resigning. He was soon followed by his faithful servant, Willie Ross. The new Prime Minister, Jim Callaghan, appointed the pro-devolutionary Bruce Millan as Secretary of State for Scotland. He in turn delegated much of the detail to a young, up-and-coming advocate, John Smith.

Partly as a result of the SLP's critique, the new Labour team beefed up *Our Changing Democracy* with a supplementary White Paper in August 1976, which removed the Secretary of State's right to control areas of dispute, passing it instead to a judicial committee of the Privy Council. The assembly was to be given control over the SDA, but denied the power to surcharge the rates. When a Bill based on these proposals was finally put to the House of Commons in November 1976, it linked Scotland and Wales, in spite of the great differences in their situations. The Bill's parliamentary journey was stormy from the start. It faced constant fire from Labour backbenchers, marshalled by Tam Dalyell, an old Etonian and socialist aristocrat.

For the tenacious Dalyell, opposition to devolution became a personal crusade. In his book, *Devolution: The End of Britain*, he poured scorn on devolution as a hastily cobbled together response to the rise of nationalism which would inevitably lead to huge tensions between Scotland and England and eventually separation.

Dalyell urged the Scots to grow up, noting caustically: 'We Scots are unsurpassed when it comes to making a mountain of invective out of some molehill of a slight, or an unintentional slight upon us.' Devolution was bad politics designed to deal with wounded dignity.

Dalyell posed the now famous West Lothian question on the role of Scottish MPs after devolution which has dogged the issue ever since. For him the point remains clear and unanswered: 'It is the issue of whether those who are elected to represent Linlithgow or Livingston can vote on the most sensitive matters that concern Liverpool and Leeds – that is, health, education and housing – and at the same time not be able to vote on those same matters in relation to Linlithgow or Livingston. It is a great difficulty.' And how much worse would the problem be if different political parties ruled in Edinburgh and London?

The bill also faced opposition from the Conservatives. Francis Pym, the shadow Cabinet member with responsibility for devolution, had devised an ingenious policy. The Conservatives argued they were in favour of the principle of devolution but opposed to this particular bill. This allowed Pym to keep both pro-and anti-devolutionists in line and keep maximum pressure on the government.

But in December 1976, the Conservatives had to choose. Callaghan's majority had been wiped out by the SLP defections and a series of by-election defeats.

On becoming Tory leader, Margaret Thatcher at first went along with party policy on promoting Scottish devolution, but soon changed her mind. On this occasion, the lady was for turning.

The Tories scented blood and imposed a three-line whip against the second reading of the Scotland and Wales Bill, knowing this would destroy the bill and also hoping it might take the government with it. Alick Buchanan-Smith and Malcolm Rifkind refused to accept this manoeuvre for, as Rifkind argued: 'Scotland is the only country with a legal system, but without a legislature to improve, modernise and amend.' They both resigned their frontbench positions and voted with the government. Another 40 Conservative MPs abstained An anti-reform duo, Teddy Taylor and Alex Fletcher, took over the top Scottish jobs.

Taylor has no doubts why he was brought in: 'It certainly seemed to me that Mrs Thatcher regarded devolution as a load of rubbish and, more important, as rather dangerous rubbish as well. And the facts are pretty obvious. If you have an assembly with tax-raising powers, it would create terrible economic problems for Scotland. If you have an assembly without tax-raising powers, then the sad fact is that all the problems of Scotland would be blamed on Whitehall. I've got a feeling I was brought into the Shadow Cabinet not because of my great abilities or enthusiasm, but simply because I was the one Scot who could be relied upon to fight against devolution in the Shadow Cabinet, which at that time was very much in favour of it.'

The Scotland and Wales Bill survived, but only after the government conceded referendums in both countries. The precedent of plebiscites had been set in 1975 with a referendum on continued membership of the EEC. In the case of devolution, it suited both the Labour leadership and its backbench critics. As with Europe, the leadership used it as a way of avoiding a damaging split in Labour ranks. And the critics used it as a delaying device, while they explored the inconsistencies in the government's proposals.

Callaghan tried to shorten the tortuous progress of the devolution bill by introducing a guillotine motion on further debate. In February 1977 this was thrown out by 312 votes to 283. The tabloids reacted with outrage and one opinion poll in the *Sunday Mail* put SNP support at 36%. The government faced a vote of 'no confidence', and possibly a heavy defeat in an election.

But the Liberals came to the rescue. In March 1977 the government offered the Liberals a deal. In return for their support in the Commons, Labour would consult them on all legislation, concede direct elections to the European parliament with a free vote on proportional representation, and involve them in the devolution legislation. The Liberals agreed. They had come through a traumatic time, during which their leader, Jeremy Thorpe, had been accused of conspiracy to murder his alleged homosexual lover. The subsequent trial traumatised the party and froze all its political activities. Though acquitted, Thorpe stood down as leader. Borders MP David Steel took his place, determined finally to make his party a political player – to give it a taste of real power.

Critics of the Lib-Lab pact believe the Liberals gave too much and got too little. David Steel still thinks they are wrong: 'I am convinced the Lib-Lab pact was the right thing both for the country and the party at that time. People in retrospect forget one very important thing. This was not an agreement between two parties freshly after an election. There was no question of arguing about the formation of a government. The government was already there. The government was in deep financial difficulties. The inflation rate was something over 20% at that time and by putting together a parliamentary support arrangement, not a coalition, we were able to get inflation down to between 7 and 8 % in the course of 18 months, and that was a tremendous achievement.'

The Liberal influence was clearly felt in one area – a new devolution bill for Scotland. This one was separated from legislation for Wales and was more radical than before. The Scottish assembly would get a block grant set for a number of years, on a percentage formula set by an independent committee. And a joint council of the UK government, and the assembly executive would work together to resolve contentious areas.

Even so, the second parliamentary struggle was no less bitter and draining. On 25 January, 1978 – Burns' Night – George Cunningham, a Scot who was the Labour MP for Islington in London, succeeded in passing an amendment which read: 'If it appears to the Secretary of State that less than 40% of the persons entitled to vote in the referendum have voted "yes" . . . he shall lay before Parliament the draft of an Order in Council for the repeal of this Act.' Political scientists now rate this the most significant backbench intervention in British politics since the war.

The Scotland Act finally staggered through the Commons in February 1978 by 313 to 287, with 11 Labour MPs voting against it – Tam Dalyell the only Scot. After 23 bills since 1887, the Commons had passed a Scottish home rule measure. Now it was up to the Scottish people.

Devolution Defeated

In Scotland, Labour tried to deal with the threat of the SNP in traditional fashion – by spending money. As well as the establishment of the SDA, the government

Labour's response to the nationalist upsurge was to throw money at Scottish causes, including the funding of the ill-fated Scottish Daily News *worker's co-operative*

Michael Foot addresses the Scottish Labour conference in Perth in March 1977. The party's pact with the Liberals, forged that month, was to edge Labour to a more radical devolution position.

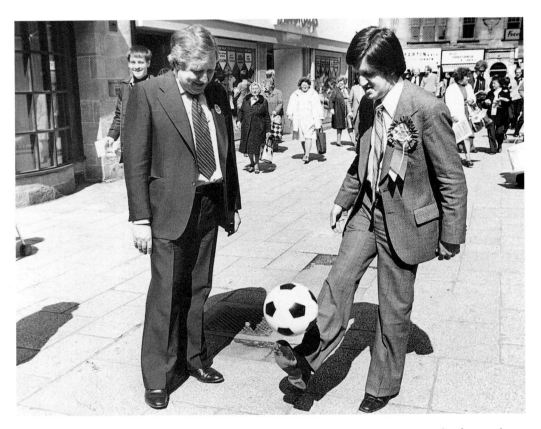

A decade after Winnie Ewing's triumph at Hamilton, the town was again the setting for a crunch by-election. This time, in 1978, Labour's George Robertson – seen playing keepie-up with Roy Hattersley – beat the SNP's Margo MacDonald.

bailed out the Linwood car plant to the tune of £600 million in 1976. It also funded the *Scottish Daily News*, a workers co-operative which took over the presses of the failed *Scottish Daily Express*. It was a short-lived experiment, with the paper closing later the same year, but it symbolised Labour's determination to be seen to be sensitive to the needs of ordinary Scots.

Labour dusted down its Scottish credentials. At its annual Scottish conference in 1977, Willie Ross made a speech asserting the party had been in favour of home rule since 1945. As Hugo Young of the *Sunday Times* put it: 'He re-wrote autobiography with a passion that would make even a member of the Politburo blush.'

The Nationalist tide, however, was already starting to turn. The SNP reached its high-water mark in the district elections of May 1977, gaining 107 seats while Labour lost 129. But in the Garscadden by-election in April 1978, a seat where the

Malcolm Rifkind was a Tory enthusiast for devolution, and resigned from the Tory front bench in protest at the party's growing opposition to home rule in the late 1970s. He campaigned for a Yes in the 1979 referendum. Later, as Scottish Secretary, he would describe himself as a federalist.

SNP had won all the wards the previous year, Labour's Donald Dewar triumphed. A month later, trade union official George Robertson defeated Margo MacDonald in Hamilton, the scene of the SNP's greatest triumph a decade before.

Robertson has no doubts about the reason for his success: 'We labelled them separatists to get away from this friendly, self-government, home rule approach which had been so useful to them in the past. We dissected their policies. We produced a document called *The Economics Of Separatism* which was quite devastating, and really got through to people they were not friendly, home rule people that were in favour of Scotland as a good romantic entity, but were actually going to break up the UK, which would be very damaging to individual people if they had got away with it.'

Tam Dalyell was the scourge of devolutionists.
A staunch Unionist, the Labour MP persistently pointed out inconsistencies in
home rule plans, arguing the dangers of playing around with parliamentary
sovereignty. His famous West Lothian question has remained a thorn in
the devolutionists' side for 20 years.

MacDonald thinks she lost for more prosaic reasons: 'There were a number of things happening in the late 1970s which meant the SNP could hardly have hoped really to stay ahead of the game. There were really pressing economic problems on practically every family in the country. And so therefore people, when they are under that sort of pressure, are not going to discuss the finer points of whether or not you are going to have devolution, whether or not you are going to have a federal system , a confederal system or whatever. You are concerned about your job.'

Referendum polling day was set for 1 March, 1979. The campaign opened against a backdrop of declining nationalist sentiment. From the start it differed from the EEC referendum four years earlier. The government provided no money for information leaflets, no television broadcasts and no support for cross-party umbrella organisations.

No restrictions on spending meant the advantage lay with the 'No' cam-

The SNP's Margo MacDonald makes her referendum view plain outside the parliament building on Edinburgh's Calton Hill. The SNP called for a Yes vote in 1979, but resented having to campaign for a Labour policy. Afterwards, many Nationalists vowed never again to campaign for anything less than independence.

The 40% rule in the referendum meant that those who failed to vote would effectively be voting No, a message taken to the streets of Dundee by this sandwich-board campaigner.

paign as leading campaigner Lord Goold acknowledges: 'There was no money washing about, but if we had a specific reason for raising money we were able to do so because people, particularly businessmen and industrialists, were so afraid of what a Scottish assembly would do to industry in Scotland, to the prospects for employment, they were prepared to put their money where their mouth was.'

And then there was the 40% rule. The referendum on EEC membership in 1975 had required no such hurdle, which was just as well as only 38% of the electorate had favoured continued membership.

The Yes side was hopelessly split. 'The Labour Says Yes' campaign would not talk to the SNP 'Yes' campaign, and both were suspicious of the two cross-party movements, 'Yes For Scotland' and the 'Alliance For An Assembly'. Local Liberal parties ran their own show and even a tiny Conservative 'Yes' campaign based in Glasgow existed independently. It was a shambles. But more important than these organisational splits, a contradiction lay at the heart of the 'Yes' cam-

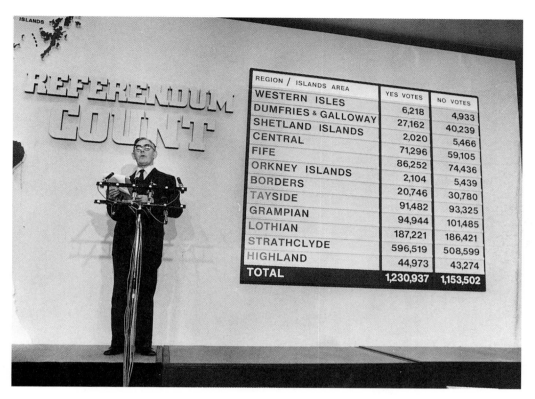

REGION / ISLANDS AREA	YES VOTES	NO VOTES
WESTERN ISLES	6,218	4,933
DUMFRIES & GALLOWAY	27,162	40,239
SHETLAND ISLANDS	2,020	5,466
CENTRAL	71,296	59,105
FIFE	86,252	74,436
ORKNEY ISLANDS	2,104	5,439
BORDERS	20,746	30,780
TAYSIDE	91,482	93,325
GRAMPIAN	94,944	101,485
LOTHIAN	187,221	186,421
STRATHCLYDE	596,519	508,599
HIGHLAND	44,973	43,274
TOTAL	**1,230,937**	**1,153,502**

One of the most striking aspects of the 1979 referendum result was that opposition tended to grow the further you travelled from the Central Belt. Many Scots, it seemed, distrusted rule from Edinburgh as much as rule from London.

paign. Labour and the Liberals argued that the Scotland Act would satisfy the Scots, safeguard a happier and more balanced Union and stop the Nationalists dead in their tracks. The SNP contended a 'Yes' vote was the first step in an inevitable path to independence.

The No campaign had no such worries. After years of vacillation the Tories nailed their colours firmly to the anti-home rule mast – the 1978 Scottish Conservative conference voted overwhelmingly to 'campaign vigorously' for a no vote. The well-funded 'Scotland Says No' campaign, backed fully by the Conservatives, ran effectively on the themes of over-government and over-taxation. A small but vocal 'Labour Says No' campaign run by Tam Dalyell, Robin Cook and Brian Wilson meant many Labour voters could rest easy about opposing their party and government.

But most important of all to the result was what became known as the 'Winter of Discontent'. Throughout the winter of 1978-79 Britain was rocked by a series of public sector strikes. At one point even the dead went unburied. The

Turnbull's cartoon in the Glasgow Herald *summed up the despondent mood
in the aftermath of the referendum. Scotland, the cowardly lion,
was too feart to take control of its own affairs.*

It was the SNP who dealt the final blow to Jim Callaghan's premiership, a move he famously described as 'turkeys voting for an early Christmas'. Under his arm is a toy Scottie dog given to him on a visit to Scotland.

public felt angry and bruised, and ill-disposed to the government that was urging them to vote yes.

In one final blow to the Yes campaign, former Prime Minister Lord Home entered the debate with a late plea to Scots to vote no, promising a better devolution scheme under a future Conservative government. He argued a no vote did not imply any disloyalty to the principle of devolution but was merely the rejection of a flawed act.

Eventually on 1 March, the voters went to the polls. On a miserable day, 62.9% of the electorate turned out. 51.6% voted yes, 48.4% voted no. But this slim majority for change represented only 32.9% of the electorate, considerably less that the Cunningham amendment required. In an old electoral roll, those electors who had died or moved house had effectively voted no. But the closeness of the result meant the devolution dream of the 1970s was dead, regardless of the brief clamour of an SNP-inspired 'Scotland Said Yes' campaign. Neither the politicians nor the public had the appetite for more debate.

For Malcolm Rifkind, one of the most prominent Tory devolutionists, the result could not have been clearer: 'I think we got it wrong. The previous two or three years had all been based on the assumption there was an irresistible demand for devolution, for a Scottish assembly. Up until then we had had opinion polls. When it came to a real referendum, when people knew their decision would actually count, one-third of Scots voted yes, one-third voted no and one-third didn't even bother to vote. I remember the following day, as soon as the results were known, I said: "That's it." If two-thirds of Scots aren't interested in supporting devolution then there is no basis for a fundamental constitutional change which would affect the UK as a whole and does not even have support in Scotland.'

Labour was left licking its wounds. John Smith, the Labour frontbencher most responsible for the devolution scheme, felt bitterly disappointed: 'It wasn't Scotland's finest hour. And I think the politicians do feel a little bit resentful about the fact that people say they want things but when they get near the point of decision they start to worry. There is a sort of ambiguity in the Scot which is puzzling at times and I felt that quite strongly then. After all, they were urging us forward and yet when we needed their help, their crucial help, in the referendum, there was some of it withheld'.

The drama had one last act. The SNP refused Labour's offer of all-party talks. In Callaghan's memorable phrase, 'like turkeys voting for an early Christmas', the SNP tabled a motion of no confidence. It succeeded by one vote. An election was called for May. The SNP were reduced from 11 MPs to two and Margaret Thatcher swept to power. The curtain closed on the devolutionary decade, and opened on the Thatcherite 1980s.

CHAPTER FOUR

DOOMSDAY DELAYED

The Thatcher Agenda

Margaret Thatcher swept into power with missionary zeal. Her philosophy was clear and uncompromising: Britain had to change and she was the woman to do it. She spelt out why in a Conservative Party political broadcast: 'Let me give you my vision. A man's right to work as he will, to spend what he earns, to own property, to have the State as servant and not as master. These are the British inheritance. They are the essence of a free economy and on that freedom all our other freedoms depend.'

As in the 1950s, Scottish politics in the early 1980s was dominated by British events. Thatcher set out an agenda which featured tax cuts, strict limits on the trades unions and privatisation of the nationalised industries. Scotland had to sign up too.

Under Thatcher, there would be no further handouts to ailing or uncompetitive businesses. And that spelled the end for many of Scotland's traditional industries. One by one the foundations of Scotland's manufacturing base crumbled. Much of Scotland's shipbuilding was lost. Factories brought to Scotland in the 1950s and 1960s through the regional planning policies of both Conservative and Labour governments closed their gates: British Leyland's truck plant at Bathgate, the Linwood car factory, the Corpach pulp mill and the Invergordon aluminium smelter. The markets were to decide and they did not like the look of Scotland. Scottish unemployment rocketed while the south of England prospered.

Political opponents and 'wets' within her own party squealed at the social consequences of her tough policies, but Thatcher was unrepentant. She had learned a grim lesson from Ted Heath's about-turn in economic policy in the early 1970s and was determined the same would not happen to her. At the Conservative Conference in 1981 she declared: 'You turn if you want to; the lady's not for turning.'

The man who had the unenviable task of carrying Thatcherism's banner in Scotland was George Younger, the new Secretary of State. He was a charming,

The man with the unenviable job of introducing Thatcherism to the Scots was George Younger, and he tried to provide spoonfuls of sugar to help the medicine go down. Younger dug in his heels with Thatcher over the closure of Ravenscraig, threatening to resign.

avuncular, old-school Conservative, liked and respected by colleagues and adversaries alike. He tried his best to soften Thatcherism for local consumption: 'I don't really accept that I in any way didn't operate the same policy as the rest of the government. But I do think that I presented it differently. I was always concerned that when something had to happen, even when it was something very regrettable like, for instance, the closure of Linwood, or the closure of the pulp mill, or the closure of the smelter, it was absolutely no use hitting it head on to the population. You've got to go and listen to what people think, you've got to take their views, you've got to give them every opportunity to bring suggestions for other solutions.'

But Younger could be tough when he chose, as first Lothian regional council, and then Stirling and Edinburgh district councils found to their cost when they tried to flout Tory spending rules. Younger used his new powers to cap their spending and order a reduction in rates. He made sure there would be no repeat of the councils' defiance of the early 1970s.

Even so, he still saw himself as Scotland's man in the Cabinet, ensuring

Workers leave a mass meeting at the Talbot car factory at Linwood, after being told the plant is to close. Thatcher believed such factories had to stand on their own feet without government help.

Scotland was getting its slice of the UK cake. He once boasted that 70% of Scots lived in assisted areas and 35 % in special development areas. And he put his foot down over the Scottish steel industry. If Ravenscraig went, so would he. Younger's resignation threat in 1982 kept Ravenscraig open – at least for a while.

There was, of course, no question of home rule. One of Thatcher's first moves was to repeal the Scotland Act in June 1979. From then, the Conservatives concentrated on what they called 'real devolution', giving council tenants the right to buy their own home, allowing parents to choose schools, and selling shares in state companies. Between 1982 and 1988, the Scottish Grand Committee did meet 17 times in Edinburgh, but a Scottish parliament it certainly was not.

Younger's general approach was to keep his head down, ride out the storm, and wait for things to improve for the economy and the Conservatives. He was a master of the quiet life, and was allowed to enjoy this courtesy of a Scottish opposition divided, demoralised and determined to fight internal battles rather than wage war on the Tories.

An Opposition Divided

The 1979 referendum result and the subsequent general election demoralised Scotland's opposition parties. The SNP felt the pain most keenly – its two MPs were a forlorn reminder of the glory days of the mid-1970s. Nationalists bickered endlessly about the way forward.

The SNP's political image was tarnished by the appearance of Siol Nan Gaidheal, the Seed of the Gael, a group of young nationalists who adopted a

quasi-paramilitary look. It was a bizarre collection of individuals from the margins of the traditionalist wing of the SNP who affected a cartoonish vision of nationalism – all highland dress and bagpipes, drummers and dirks – burning Union Jacks, and trying to look like a militia. But the SNG was an embarrassment rather than a real threat to the SNP.

Of deeper concern to the leadership was the '79 Group, a SNP socialist pressure group which included in its ranks Margo MacDonald, the former SLP leader Jim Sillars and a young Alex Salmond. The group urged Scots to 'join the Scottish resistance', and campaigned vigorously for a Scottish socialist republic.

Salmond is clear about how the '79 Group thought the SNP had to change: 'It had to have a label, an ideological label. The people had to know what kind of party it was, not in terms of streams of policy documents, but in terms of owning up to a political identity. And the centrepiece of what the '79 Group were arguing was that the SNP should adopt and own up to a political identity, and that identity should be on the left-of-centre.'

The SNP acted in 1982 to expel 'fringe groups'. This lumped together the socialist 79 Group, which included future leader Alex Salmond, and Siol Nan Gaidheal, which had a liking for paramilitary trappings.

By 1981, the group was powerful and popular enough to get members onto the SNP national executive. Sillars, elected as SNP vice-chairman, called for civil disobedience. It was an audacious call to arms, but very few of the SNP foot soldiers took it up. In October, Sillars and a handful of supporters tried to occupy the Royal High School building, the proposed home of the Scottish parliament on Calton Hill in Edinburgh, in order to stage a debate on unemployment. But nationalist sentiment was moribund and the Scottish public had little appetite for civil disobedience.

The new SNP leader, Gordon Wilson, a conservative Dundee lawyer, tried vainly to maintain party discipline. Activists ignored his calls for unity. Matters finally came to a head at the 1982 SNP conference in Ayr. Wilson called for a ban on all internal factions, the SNG and '79 Group included, and threatened to resign if he was defeated.

He is still adamant he was right: 'We had a position of a power-vacuum and anarchy and that could not be tolerated. But it went on for something like two years before eventually corrective action had to be taken. I took an immediate decision to do that, and put my whole political career at risk on that, simply because I felt the party would fall apart unless some action were taken.'

Many activists stormed out of the conference hall, but the motion was carried, and the groups eventually disbanded after a bitter struggle. Alex Salmond and six others were thrown out of the party for trying to carry on the aims of the '79 Group under the guise of the all-party Scottish Socialist Society, although the expulsions were eventually downgraded to suspensions. This in-fighting paralysed the SNP as a political movement and left a legacy of personal distrust still felt in the party more than a decade later.

The early 1980s were a parallel disaster for the Labour Party. The far-left Trotskyist Militant Tendency succeeded in taking over the Young Socialists, Labour's youth wing, and infiltrating many moribund constituency Labour parties. Although they got short shrift in Scotland, Militant's activities gave the right-wing tabloid press a field day on 'loony left' activities.

But Labour's most serious wound was self-inflicted. Stunned by defeat in 1979, the party swung far to the left. At its 1980 conference it adopted a platform of unilateral nuclear disarmament, withdrawal from the EEC and removing the power of the MPs to select the leader. The party's choice of Michael Foot rather than Denis Healey to replace Jim Callaghan as leader proved equally disastrous. In an era of increasingly presidential-style politics, Foot cut a poor figure beside Thatcher. The Labour right was despondent.

In January 1981, Labour called a special conference at Wembley to decide how to pick future leaders. Led by Tony Benn, the left successfully reduced MPs to 30% of the new electoral college. It was the final straw for many on the right. The Gang of Four – David Owen, Shirley Williams, Roy Jenkins and Bill

Thatcher's politics were regarded as alien by most Scots. There was also an element of personal dislike in the Scottish public's reaction to her, something that the SNP made good use of in its posters.

Rodgers – issued the Limehouse Declaration advocating a Council for Social Democracy. On 13 March, Labour MPs and one Conservative MP formed the Social Democratic Party which favoured PR, a Freedom of Information Act, support for the EEC, NATO and Scottish devolution. Although it lacked party workers and a national structure, the SDP brought many fresh and enthusiastic recruits into politics.

It had little initial impact in Scotland because the Labour right were traditional Labour loyalists and the Bennite left was much less influential. For example, in March 1982, under the new rules of selection, not one Scottish MP had been deselected at the first round. Also as Charles Kennedy, who would win Ross, Cromarty and Skye for the SDP in 1983, puts it: 'The minimal nature of the Labour defections to the Alliance in Scotland I think in part was a reflection of the fact that the Labour Party was a lot more sane in Scotland. Unlike the Labour Party, particularly in London, but in other parts of England as well, Labour was a party of government and therefore of responsibility.'

Indeed John Smith felt Labour in Scotland saved the British Labour Party: 'The early 1980s were dark days for the Labour Party. I remember walking away from the Wembley conference very disconsolate about the future of the party and feeling it was pulling itself apart. But very few Scots actually did anything as foolish as to leave the party. I think the Labour Party owes a great debt to Scotland, because we were the ballast, we held the ground, the necessary ground, during the years in which the Labour Party faced up to its problems.'

For a time it seemed the breakaway party would succeed in its ambition of breaking the mould of British politics. Liberal leader David Steel was keen to woo these challengers for the centre ground in British politics: 'Throughout the entire birth process of the SDP, my approach was publicly to embrace them, smother them with love and assume a putative alliance.' He got his way.

In June 1981, the SDP struck an alliance with the Liberals and released a joint set of principles, *A Fresh Start For Britain*. David Steel boldly told the UK Liberals at their conference 'Go back to your constituencies and prepare for government'.

In September, the flow of Labour MPs to the SDP was stemmed when Denis Healey won the deputy leadership of the Party after a bruising struggle with Tony Benn. Healey won by less than 1%. If he had lost the Labour Party could easily have fractured.

Even so, the new Alliance surged ahead with a series of by-election triumphs. In October William Pitt, a Liberal, won the Croydon Northwest by-election from the Conservatives. In November, Shirley Williams won Crosby for the SDP with a 25% swing also from the Conservatives. A poll in December gave the Alliance 50.5% of the vote compared to 23.5% for Labour and 23% for the Conservatives.

The next by-election test was in Scotland, and it was something special. In

Roy Jenkins scored a famous victory for the SDP in the Hillhead by-election. But the new party's membership in Scotland was limited, largely because Labour north of the border was seen as more moderate than in England.

March 1982, Roy Jenkins travelled north to do battle for the hearts and minds of the voters of Glasgow Hillhead. He remembers the excitement of the occasion well: 'We had great meetings throughout the campaign. Perhaps the greatest was in Hyndland secondary school when we had a great overflow crowd in the play-ground. It was a frosty, moonlit, slightly misty night and over a thousand people remained in the playground outside. And all the speakers – the whole of the Gang of Four – came and spoke. Each of us came out and addressed them one by one, having done the meeting inside. And I think perhaps that was the time I thought maybe we were going to win after all.'

The next day he travelled north to the Scottish Liberal conference in St Andrews. Menzies Campbell, later Liberal Democrat MP for North East Fife, recalls the heady mood of the time. 'The atmosphere was truly electric. I think only two or three times in my life have the hairs stood up on the back of my neck

Michael Forsyth enjoyed a close relationship with Thatcher, who once called him her 'young Lochinvar'. He was in the vanguard of the Thatcherite revolution in Scotland, a position that put him in conflict with moderates such as Malcolm Rifkind.

like that. And when Roy Jenkins came into the town hall at St Andrews, people went mad. All the sort of reserve you normally expect just went out of the window. It was like a Hollywood production, believing that anything was possible, that somehow the Alliance – the Liberals and the SDP – there was no political obstacle it could not overcome.'

With the SNP and Labour in disarray, it seemed only the Alliance could successfully challenge Thatcher. Eight days after the Hillhead by-election, the Argentinians invaded the Falklands. David Steel believes the invasion's impact can hardly be exaggerated.

'How might the political history of this country have been different if a remote South American dictator hadn't landed two or three people in some rocky islands in South Georgia off the Falklands. That triggered the Falklands conflict, the restoration of Mrs Thatcher's prestige as a national leader – because her stock was very low before that, people forget that – and the elimination of

Mick McGahey, Communist leader of the NUM in Scotland, was a totem of the Scottish left over three decades. In the 1960s he had been influential in persuading the STUC to campaign for a Scottish parliament.

domestic politics for about a year. And it killed the momentum of the Alliance.'

Thatcher called a general election in June 1983, still basking in the glow of the British nationalism unleashed during the Falklands War. Labour offered *New Hope For Britain*, a highly detailed left-wing manifesto dubbed by Gerald Kaufman, 'the longest suicide note in history'.

The election was a disaster for Labour. It polled just 27.6%, its lowest vote since 1918, lost 119 deposits and won just 209 seats. The Alliance suffered from the vagaries of the first-past-the post system, its 25.4% of the vote returning only 23 MPs, eight of them in Scotland.

The Falklands factor worked in Scotland too. The Conservatives, despite the economic gloom, only dropped 3% in the polls and lost one seat, still leaving them with 21 seats and a firm position as Scotland's second party. The SNP was still in the electoral doldrums, polling just 11.7% of the vote, its worst showing since 1970, though the party hung on to its two MPs.

*Pickets try to stop the car of a working miner at Bilston Glen
during the coal strike in 1984.*

Labour returned 41 Scottish MPs. There were brief, dark rumblings among a few Labour MPs about a 'Scottish Mandate' and possible parliamentary disruption, but this soon fizzled out. The Labour leadership would not countenance treating the Scottish result any differently from the English one. Overall, Thatcher had triumphed with a huge majority of 144. The Iron Lady seemed invincible.

Thatcher stepped up the pace of her reforms. The unions in general, and the miners in particular, were firmly in her sights. The miners were the most militant union, and their leader, Arthur Scargill, was a hero to much of the left. Defeat Scargill, and the battle against trades union power would be over.

In February 1984, the miners struck against pit closures. It was the beginning of one of the most bitter and prolonged industrial disputes Britain had ever known. Thatcher, having watched the miners destroy Ted Heath, refused to budge. Scargill refused to call a ballot, and tried to encourage all the miners to come out with massive secondary picketing, resulting in bloody stand-offs with the police. In Nottingham, the Union of Democratic Mineworkers formed, and kept on working. Miner fought miner, until the NUM called off industrial action in March 1985.

For the new Labour leader, Neil Kinnock, who had taken over from Michael Foot, this was a difficult start. The Labour leadership had to choose between its instinctive sympathy with the miners and its hatred of 'Scargillism'. To Kinnock, himself a miner's son, parliament was the legitimate means of opposition to Conservative policy, and he had no time for the 'guerrilla tactics' and sometimes illegal methods of the NUM and its supporters on the left. The government won the day, the trades unions were cowed.

Kinnock redoubled his efforts to make Labour electable. He jettisoned his left sympathies and turned savagely on Militant. Anyone in 'a party within a party' was to be expelled. Kinnock knew Labour had to modernise to win the next election. The party was not trusted by the voters, especially in the English south-east, and the key electoral battleground of the Midlands where many embraced the Thatcher revolution.

The Doomsday Election

Kinnock's tentative reform of the Labour Party paid dividends in Scotland. In the face of the Thatcher revolution it was to Labour that the Scots turned to for help. Every election in the mid 1980s revealed the deepening unpopularity of the Thatcher government. The June 1984 European elections saw Labour take five seats and 41% of the vote. The regional elections two years later were a catastrophe for the Conservatives – Labour took 43.9%, and won majorities in Fife, Lothian, Central and Strathclyde. Increasingly, Labour were the establishment party in the central belt of Scotland – a thin layer of resistance between Scotland and the rule of Westminster.

As the Thatcher government pressed ahead with rolling back the state and encouraging individual initiative, it was perhaps inevitable that its popularity would suffer in Scotland where the state was more entrenched in day-to-day economic life. A strong selfish element aided Labour's dominance, the Conservatives lost the votes not only of those reliant on state aid, but also the disproportionately large numbers who administered it, nicknamed the 'salariat'. A stronger factor was a deep-seated Scottish belief in the value of community. Thatcher may have believed there was no such thing as society – Scotland disagreed.

The biggest body blow to the Scottish Conservatives in the 1980s was the poll tax. In the spring of 1985 local authorites set new rates, a reassessment postponed from 1983 due to the reform of local government funding. The huge rates proposed sent shock-waves throughout the Conservative establishment in Scotland.

Contrary to popular belief, it was not Margaret Thatcher's idea to impose the poll tax on Scots first, she was begged to do so by the Scottish Tory party. These Conservative activists make their view clear at the Tory conference in Perth in 1985.

The screams from the suburbs were deafening. Home owners – the traditional Tory power base – were facing increases of up to 40% in their domestic rates. Conservative leaders feared an electoral disaster if the party had to fight the next election with this millstone round its neck. So the poll tax, devised by Scottish right-wing radicals like Douglas Mason to offer an alternative funding of local government, was born. The logic was simple. Everyone used local government services, therefore everyone should pay – equally – for them, be they millionaire or miner.

Tories north of the border pushed for it to be brought in early in Scotland. Conservatives were desperate to fight the next general election on the grounds of abolishing the punitive new rates. Thatcher, often criticised for trying out the poll tax on the Scots, agreed. By May 1987, she was able to announce that the poll tax would be introduced in April of the following year. The Scottish Tories had their wish. They had their flagship policy for the election.

They also had a new leader. When Michael Heseltine walked out of the Cabinet over the Westland affair in 1986, it had an unexpected knock-on effect in Scotland. George Younger was promoted to the Ministry of Defence and Malcolm Rifkind replaced him at the Scottish Office. A more waspish debater than Younger, Rifkind was keen to go on the offensive. He was less inclined to boast about the amount of money he was bringing to Scotland, feeling that was dancing to the opposition's tune, and instead stressed the improvements free market reforms were bringing to the Scottish economy. But even Rifkind's debating skills struggled to contain the rising anger as people realised what the poll tax would mean to them.

In the June 1987 general election, Kinnock's Labour Party continued to improve its British postition. But the party was still vulnerable, particularly on defence, and the electorate still suspicious of the power of the left. Despite Hugh Hudson's ground-breaking party political broadcast featuring the Kinnocks – dubbed 'Neil and Glenys – The Movie', Labour struggled against the feel-good factor and conspicuous wealth in the Tory heartlands of the South of England. Voters who had bought their own homes saw their value multipy. The new shareowners enjoyed fat dividends. Thatcher romped home with a majority of 102.

The one blight on the Tory victory was Scotland. The Conservative losses were stark. The party lost 11 of its 21 MPs, its worst result in Scotland since 1910. The Conservatives took 24% of the vote which meant their support had more than halved since 1955.

Labour won an extra nine seats and the Alliance and SNP another each. Labour now had 50 of the 72 seats in Scotland, a feat unparalleled since the great Liberal victories early in the century. It was a fantastic result, but what were they going to do with it? Alex Salmond, newly elected SNP MP for Banff and Buchan was quick to put the pressure on them, christening them 'the feeble 50'.

This shocking defeat led to a prolonged bout of Conservative soul searching as the party struggled to make sense of such a massive rejection. Conservatives put forward a series of reasons for their defeat – many of them contradictory. A post-election report by the vice-presidents of the Scottish Conservative and Unionist Association confirmed the party was perceived as English and anti-Scottish, and later Conservative research showed the Scots considered Thatcher 'hard'.

For the Conservative right, the prescription was a greater dose of the medicine to make the patient better. Right-winger Michael Forsyth argued the Scots had not yet experienced the full benefit of market reforms. Give them time and they would come round. Chancellor Nigel Lawson travelled to Scotland and lambasted the Scots' continuing addiction to the 'dependency culture'.

The sinking ship: A clutch of leading Scottish Tories prepare for a Thames regatta in the mid-1980s. It was a period of relentless decline for the party in Scotland. Left to right: Michael Forsyth, Michael Hirst, John MacKay, Allan Stewart, Lord Cameron, Gerald Malone, Lord James Douglas-Hamilton and Peter Fraser.

The left of the party disagreed. Alick Buchanan-Smith refused to take ministerial office under Thatcher after the 1987 general election, and was candid about his reasons: 'We were not paying sufficent attention to what ordinary people were thinking and feeling, and secondly, some of those things that have been of great value to us in Scotland over the generations and even over the centuries – we have always given a higher rating to them – such as education, such as the social services – people had a sense they were perhaps not been given the priority they should have been given.'

But Rifkind himself believed the political rewards of popular Conservative policies would come – in time. For the first time since the war, the majority of Scots now owned their own homes. 'If someone was buying their council house in Falkirk or Glasgow or Motherwell, I think there was a degree of uncertainty as to whether they were letting the side down, using the policy of a Conservative government. Therefore I think it takes a little while before people examine their political allegiance and which political party best represents their interests.'

The Conservatives even reconsidered home rule, debating it at their 1988 conference. The Conservative Constitutional Reform Forum led by Struan Stevenson, Brian Meek and Michael Fry, suggested the Conservatives think again on devolution. The party rejected that suggestion overwhelmingly. Welcoming the rejection, Thatcher told the conference: 'As long as I am leader of this party we shall defend the Union and reject legislative devolution unequivocally.'

Party chairman Lord Goold spelt out the bottom line for the Scottish Conservatives: 'Devolution leading to a Scottish Assembly or independence would be so wrong for Scotland that I certainly don't think we should switch sides on this. We would gain no brownie points. I think the only time we could perhaps get into a serious situation would be if we were unable to man the Scottish Office, if we did not have enough members of parliament to man the Scottish Office. I could see then that would obviously be a difficult situation and we would have to look at it. But we are not going to get into that situation.'

But many believed the problem was not the Conservative attitude to home rule, but Thatcher herself. She redoubled her efforts to appeal to the Scots insisting that they had 'invented Thatcherism' with their values of 'hard work, self-reliance, thrift and enterprise', but her words fell on stony ground. The gulf between Thatcher and the Scots was confirmed by a visit in May 1988.

She attended the General Assembly of the Church of Scotland and delivered what became famous as her 'Sermon on the Mound'. It was a dramatic speech, telling Scotland's traditionally liberal churchmen and women to pay heed to the biblical passage that says those who do not work shall not eat. She went on to highlight the key role of money: 'How could we respond to the many calls for help or invest for the future, or support the wonderful artists and craftsmen whose work also glorifies God, unless we had first worked hard and used our talents to create the necessary wealth.' The clergy was outraged. Unperturbed, Thatcher went on to attend the Scottish Cup final at Hampden where she was resoundingly booed by the collected Celtic and Dundee United fans, and shown thousands of red cards which had been handed out before the match.

Teddy Taylor felt her pain: 'I think what was wrong with poor Mrs Thatcher is that she didn't appreciate the Scots want Scots fighting for them, not a lady from London coming to hand out largesse or coming to Scottish occasions and appearing to sound Scottish. She was terribly perplexed about it. She tried everything she possibly could because she actually cared about Scotland, she liked Scotland and she became very depressed that she got nothing but abuse and negative responses when she came.'

But Charles Kennedy thinks Thatcher had a beneficial effect on Scottish politics: 'Mrs Thatcher, ironically, has maybe proved to be the greatest of all Scottish

When Thatcher came north to lecture the Church of Scotland on morality, her 'Sermon on the Mound' outraged mainstream Scottish opinion. Thatcher was puzzled and hurt by the Scots' reluctance to take Thatcherism to heart.

nationalists. This arch-unionist, hectoring figure has brought out the worst in Scotland in terms of our latent chauvinism, but it has also brought out something good and positive. She has forced the parties in Scotland and indeed the establishment in Scotland beyond politics to rethink its role, to rethink the system of decision-making in Scotland and hopefully she has propelled us in the direction of a legislative tier. So, irony of all time, we may yet have to raise a dram to Maggie for doing so much for us.'

A Nation Once Again

The 1987 election was a curtain-raiser to dramatic changes in all Scotland's opposition parties. The election had been great for the Alliance in Scotland, where it won nine seats, by far the centre's best result since the war, but poor in the UK as a whole. David Steel believed the centre could no longer hold two separate parties. He proposed marriage. David Owen preferred divorce.

Owen fought the merger tooth and nail, and has no regrets: 'I didn't want the merger because I am not a Liberal, never have been a Liberal and never want to be a Liberal. I think they are a very necessary part of politics, but thank you very much, I ain't one and I don't intend to become one. I have no particular objection to David Steel wanting to merge because a merger was a takeover and he always wanted to take over the SDP. And he fought his corner extremely well to get a merged party but it hasn't done him any good, has it? He is not the leader of the merged party.'

But the Liberals believed the central problem was Owen's ego. Menzies Campbell finds him an astonishing character. 'David Owen had, and still has, the capacity to tell you today the precise opposite of what he told you last week and to do so with the same fervour, the same degree of credibility, the same degree of honesty, I think as well. But it makes it very difficult if you are trying to operate any kind of joint or team leadership.'

The struggle over the merger paralysed the centre and sent both parties poll ratings spiralling down. In the European elections of 1989, the Liberal Democrats faced the ignominy of being pushed into fifth place in Scotland behind the Greens. The Greens took over 7% of the vote, the Liberal Democrats just over 4%. But in a reversal of the trends of the early 1980s, the disintegration of the centre was accompanied by the uniting of the Nationalists. At its 1988 conference, the SNP took two crucial decisions: it advocated a mass non-payment campaign against the poll tax and it unveiled its new flagship policy of 'Independence in Europe'.

With Independence in Europe, an independent Scotland country would forsake Westminster for a seat at the top table in Brussels. Setting aside the SNP's traditional antipathy to Europe, the new policy seemed fresh and attractive. It linked well with Europe's growing influence and its key principle of subsidiarity, which advocates the devolution of power down to the lowest practicable level.

More importantly, it allowed the SNP to seem less isolationist. Scotland would be leaving Britain but joining Europe. Immediately Nationalists became less defensive, as Winnie Ewing observes: 'We want to sit wherever the nations sit, be it in the United Nations, the Commonwealth and of course in the European Community. And we found that immediately got rid of the separatist tag. You can't go on about customs at the border if there are not going to be customs at any of the borders. You can't taunt us with that old taunt – you can't say "You want to be separate". I say we are separate at the moment – we want to participate.'

In November 1988, the SNP had a chance to test out its two new policies with a by-election at Govan, scene of Margo MacDonald's victory in 1973. This time the SNP candidate was her husband, Jim Sillars. He fought the by-election on a broad-based platform of opposition to Thatcherism – she could be defeated if five million Scots started fighting back. He won with a majority of 3,500.

An exultant Sillars addressed the crowd outside. 'It became quite plain that Mrs Thatcher wanted to take over Scotland and make it just another little bit of Tory England. The message from Govan is – you are not on.' The SNP bandwagon was rolling again.

This struck fear in the heart of the Labour Party, already struggling with the impotent 'mandate' its great victory in Scotland in 1987 had given it. Once again it was living out the so-called 'doomsday scenario' where Scotland returned an overwhelming number of Labour MPs but ended up with a Conservative government. Labour feared the voters were losing patience with this state of affairs and turning to the SNP.

Labour was now solidly pro-devolution, but that seemed irrelevant when the party had to win at Westminster first. Kinnock desperately needed the Scottish Labour vote to keep within even sniffing distance of the Conservative majority in Westminster, but he had an uneasy relationship with the Scottish party and totally misjudged its post-election mood.

At the 1988 Scottish Labour conference, he failed to mention either Labour's great election result or the issue of home rule. When challenged on TV afterwards he remarked he had not mentioned many other things, such as 'weather conditions in the Himalayas'. Many in the party were incensed.

In March 1988 Labour activists formed a new faction, Scottish Labour Action, to push for a stronger line on home rule and non-payment of the poll tax. The tax was introduced in Scotland on 1 April, 1988 to popular fury, and Labour held a special conference in September to consider its position. The conference rejected non-payment, with shadow Secretary Donald Dewar arguing that a party which wanted to be the government could not advocate breaking the law.

But a non-payment campaign grew regardless. Tommy Sheridan, then a Labour Party member, became unofficial leader of the campaign and of the grassroots Anti-Poll Tax Federation. In Glasgow in particular, the federation's rallies and marches were a popular focus for the public outrage. Sheridan was eventually kicked out of the Labour Party and ended up jailed for his part in preventing the warrant sales that were instigated to recoup unpaid poll tax. While in jail he was elected to Glasgow District Council as a Scottish Militant Labour councillor.

But the majority of the Scottish electorate did pay their tax and worried if non-payment would make their taxes higher. What did incense them was the government's indifference to Scottish protest, and its bowing the knee to English outrage when the tax was introduced there in 1989. Thatcher only started to waver when faced with English riots, and when English Conservative MPs felt the slimness of their majorities. As Teddy Taylor puts it: 'I get the impression the

Tensions between the two Davids, Owen and Steel, often made life uncomfortable for the Alliance in the mid-1980s. Pictured on stage at a conference in Dundee is Russell Johnston, leader of the Liberals in Scotland.

poll tax problem in Scotland was simply that the people in Scotland felt they were being used as mugs. I think the Scots probably have good reason to feel bitter that their complaints and their protests were rather brushed aside, but two bad by-elections in England and the government goes daft.'

This anger was manna for the Nationalists, so Labour redoubled its efforts to appear strong on the Scottish Question. Kinnock returned to Scotland in 1989, having learned his lesson. He reaffirmed Labour's commitment to home rule in typically verbose style: 'We hold it to be self-evident that in the capital of Scotland there shall be established a democratic, directly elected assembly to govern with the Scottish people, for the Scottish people, by the Scottish people, in Scotland.'

Labour had found a tailor-made vehicle to display its home rule credentials in the Scottish constitutional convention. The convention was the brainchild of

SNP MPs Alex Salmond and Margaret Ewing at a party conference ball.

*Miners leave the Seafield colliery cage for the last time in 1988.
The warnings of closures made by the NUM during the pit dispute
were to proved correct.*

the Campaign for a Scottish Assembly. Formed after the 1979 referendum campaign, the CSA was a cross-party campaign which kept the home rule flag flying in devolution's dog days of the early 1980s. By the late 1980s, the CSA felt the public mood was sufficiently robust to move the campaign up a gear. Faced with the 'doomsday scenario', the CSA set up a committee of 'prominent Scots' to examine home rule. In July 1988, this committee issued *A Claim of Right for Scotland*.

The document spelled out the intellectual case for a Scottish Parliament and advocated a convention of all the Scottish political parties and any other inter-

Jim Sillars returns to Westminster to the skirl of the pipes as SNP MP for Govan after his by-election victory in 1988. He became the SNP's deputy leader and fashioned the party's fundamentalist campaign in the general election. But Sillars lost the seat back to Labour in the subsequent general election.

ested groups to devise a scheme for Scotland's government.

The Conservatives, unsurprisingly, declined to take part. Labour was initially hesitant, even though, as the convention would be based on political support at the 1987 general election, it would be the largest grouping. The Liberal Democrats, Greens and Communists agreed. The big question was the attitude of the SNP.

Ironically it was SNP leader Gordon Wilson who first mooted the idea of a cross-party assembly in a bill presented to parliament in 1980. Despite initial hostility from within his own party's ranks, he finally persuaded the SNP national executive to adopt it as policy in 1984.

But, by late 1988, Sillars had triumphed at Govan and the SNP looked on the brink of an electoral upsurge. Talking about a devolutionary package seemed a distraction from the dream of Independence in Europe. After the

Poll tax campaigner Tommy Sheridan gives his own sermon on the mound. With Labour opposing non-payment, Militant found itself a role in Scottish politics.

Harry Ewing and David Steel, joint chairmen of the Scottish Constitutional Convention, sign the Claim of Right in July 1988.

first meeting of the steering committee, the SNP walked out.

This was a major public relations victory for Labour and the Liberal Democrats, who were now able to portray themselves as the parties who had Scotland's national interest at heart. The Scottish Constitutional Convention's first meeting took place in the Assembly Hall in Edinburgh on 30 March, 1989. The joint chairmen were David Steel and Harry Ewing. All of the Labour and Liberal Democrat MPs, apart from Tam Dalyell, put their signatures to the founding declaration, as did representatives of the majority of Scotland's local authorities, the STUC, the Greens, the Communists and Scotland's churches.

The convention surprised the cynics by fashioning a series of compromises over the next year as it drew up its blueprint for a Scottish parliament. Most astonishing of all, Labour conceded that this parliament would be elected by proportional representation, immediately making it more attractive to those who feared it would be dominated by Labour and the central belt. Although some key issues had been fudged, Labour and the Liberal Democrats were going into the next election with an agreed scheme for constitutional reform.

Canon Kenyon Wright, the chair of the executive committee of the convention had a response ready for the expected scorn of the iron lady: 'What happens if that other voice we all know so well responds by saying we say no. We say no and we are the state. Well, we say yes and we are the people.'

That familiar voice, however, was starting to lose its force. Beset by problems over the poll tax, rising unemployment and a disastrous split in the Conservative Party over further European integration, Thatcher's leadership seemed to be failing. As the party slipped down the polls and a general election loomed the Conservative Party turned on its leader. In November 1990, despite last-gasp pleadings by loyal supporters including Michael Forsyth, Thatcher was forced to resign. The unprepossessing John Major, who as Thatcher's favoured successor had been promoted rapidly through the posts of chief whip, Foreign Secretary and Chancellor, took over.

In Scotland, the public mood was expectant. With the Conservatives in the doldrums, a revitalised SNP and a unified home rule movement in the convention, surely one grey man couldn't stop Scotland in the 1990s finally having its parliament?

CHAPTER FIVE

STILL RESTLESS?

'Well, who'd have thought it?' John Major's opening words at his first Cabinet meeting as Prime Minister found a ready echo in the country at large. It was hard to believe Margaret Thatcher was no longer in power and stamping her imprint daily on British life. With her gone – and with the Berlin Wall breached, the Soviet Union crumbling and the cracks appearing in South African apartheid – suddenly anything seemed possible. Nowhere was this feeling stronger than in Scotland. So much of Scottish politics in the previous decade had been dominated by opposition to Thatcher and her revolution. The sense of release and potential was palpable.

For more than a year Major kept the country guessing about when he would seek a personal vote of confidence from the British people. By the time he eventually called a general election in the spring of 1992, home rule once more dominated the political agenda in Scotland. Expectations were high. The opposition parties had tasted blood in the Tories' loss of Kincardine and Deeside to the Liberal Democrats in a by-election in November 1991. Although the result was unremarkable for such a marginal constituency at that time, it took on a larger significance. As anticipation of the election grew keener, it was looked upon as an omen. Commentators began to speculate on a Tory-free Scotland after polling day.

When *The Scotsman* published an opinion poll in January suggesting an unprecedented 50% of Scots favoured independence, it confirmed the impression that Scotland could be approaching a watershed. The newspaper organised a debate with the four party leaders in the Usher Hall in Edinburgh, televised on BBC Scotland. With Labour leaders doubting the public's interest in political debate on a chilly Saturday night, they made little effort to rally their troops. So the night belonged to Alex Salmond and a legion of vocal SNP supporters who had few qualms about barracking the other speakers. The emotional charge of the event, and the interest taken by Scottish and London media alike, ensured the constitution would be centre stage in the coming general election campaign.

Union Dues

Major enjoyed a close relationship with Ian Lang, his Scottish Secretary. They had served in the whips office together in the early 1980s and had grown to like and trust one another. The advice to Downing Street from some senior Scottish Tories was that Conservative backing for some kind of devolution was probably inevitable in the long term. Major and Lang disagreed. They would make a virtue of standing on a point of principle in defence of the Union.

On a visit to Glasgow, the Prime Minister told a gathering of Tory candidates: 'It is not the Conservative Party that gains – or has gained – most from the ties

Labour's Donald Dewar underestimated the amount of interest there would be in the Great Debate early in 1992. The night belonged to the Nationalists, who had packed the Usher Hall, and the event heightened anticipation of the general election.

Neil Kinnock in confident mood at a Labour election rally in Edinburgh's Meadowbank Stadium. Election analysts would later say he lacked the full trust of the British voters, and this contributed to Labour's defeat.

between Scotland and England. And yet it is our party that supports the Union. Not because it's always been good for us, but because it has always seemed right to us. Not always in our political interest, but always in that of our kingdom and the countries within it.'

A get-out clause was also thought wise, however. So Major promised to 'take stock' of the government's attitude to Scotland after the election. No one truly expected this to lead to a wholesale conversion to devolution. But it allowed the Tories to appear in the election campaign both as defenders of the status quo and its prospective reformers, hopefully pleasing as many people as possible in the process.

On the Monday of the final week of the campaign, Major overruled Conservative Central Office and made the defence of the Union the centrepiece of the morning press conference. Central Office had wanted it to be tax, and party chairman Chris Patten thought the Prime Minister's choice 'mildly eccentric'. Major's only regret was that he had not started the entire campaign with it. The head of Major's policy unit, Sarah Hogg, would later doubt whether his defence of the Union swayed many votes in Scotland or England. But because Major obviously cared so deeply about the subject and was able to speak with passion and sincerity, his image was enhanced at a critical moment in the campaign.

On election night a prominent Scottish journalist held a party in his home in Edinburgh's Morningside, buying in a case of champagne. A bottle was to be opened every time a Scottish Tory MP lost his seat. The guests looked forward to a night of celebration as the BBC opened its election programme with a prediction of a Scottish Tory wipe-out. They eventually had to make do with Bulgarian red wine. Prime Minister John Major held on with a majority of 21 seats. And to the stunned disbelief of the Scottish opposition parties and their supporters, the night was a triumph for the Scottish Tories and, by implication, for the Union. Against the UK trend, the Tory share of the vote went up from 24% to 25.6%.

Amid acrimonious scenes in Stirling between Labour and SNP supporters, the most loathed Tory in Scotland, Michael Forsyth, scraped through by 703 votes, aided by an increased Nationalist vote. Kincardine and Deeside was again in Tory hands. And there was even a Tory gain from Labour, the only one in the UK, in Aberdeen South. As Neil Kinnock eloquently conceded defeat in London in a hoarse and heavy voice, it was the Tories who were popping the champagne corks.

The Scottish Conservatives settled back into the routine of government feeling rather pleased with themselves. In particular there was satisfaction that pressure for constitutional change had been well and truly seen off. The fact that three-quarters of the Scottish electorate voted for some degree of home rule

Major campaigning in Cupar in the run-up to the 1992 election. His rallying cry in defence of the Union is credited by some as one of the reasons for his successful re-election.

could, they believed, be safely ignored. The 'taking stock' exercise promised by Major was dutifully attended to with the publication of a White Paper, *Scotland and the Union*. Its language demonstrated a Conservative recognition of Scotland's status as a nation that had not been apparent since the late 1970s. There were expressions of worthy concern about making Scots feel less distant from the business of government. But the actual proposals were thin – an enhanced role for the little-known Scottish Grand Committee, administrative devolution of arts and training from Whitehall to the Scottish Office, and little else. In its timidity it was an eerie echo of Labour's White Paper on Scottish Affairs almost 50 years earlier. There was no concession to the central demand of the home rule movement – direct democratic accountability. The attitude of the Tory party in the aftermath of the election triumph seemed to be: Well, why should we?

Labour's George Galloway MP, seen here on a Scotland United march in Edinburgh, was rebuked by the leadership for 'collaborating' with the SNP.

People Power

In the weeks after the general election, the Scottish opposition parties had a humdinger of a hangover. The nation had drunk deeply of the intoxicating anticipation of a new government, and a price had to be paid. It was a time for regrets. The SNP received calls from penitent voters bitterly regretting they had given Labour one last chance. In Stirling, a sheepish SNP voter confessed to guilt at not voting tactically to get rid of Forsyth. The Scottish media fell into an orgy of self-doubt and breast-beating, blaming itself for inflating expectations and failing to scrutinise its own assumptions in the run-up to the poll.

Some people felt a need to do more than lick wounds. They wanted to show there was still spirit in the home rule movement, despite the defeat. Scotland United was born. This cobbled-together alliance of politicians, public relations executives, novelists and pop stars organised two successful rallies in the weeks following the defeat, attracting 5,000 people at the largest. It was a decent turnout, but hardly a popular rebellion.

Scotland United drifted into obscurity. Its chosen campaign issue – a call for a multi-option referendum on Scotland's future – had SNP backing but failed to win enthusiastic Labour support or to catch the public imagination. Another new group born in the dark hours following the defeat, the intellectually based Common Cause, also failed to connect. Only the rag-bag of assorted activists calling themselves Democracy for Scotland found themselves a lasting role as guardians of a vigil outside the parliament building on Edinburgh's Calton Hill.

The Labour Party leadership in Scotland was chary of these attempts at cross-party politics. It was for them a breach of party discipline. And perhaps they saw it, rightly, as an indictment of their failure to achieve anything for Scotland through the usual system of party rivalries. When George Galloway, Labour's flamboyant Glasgow Hillhead MP, met senior SNP figures shortly after the election to talk about anti-government strategy, he was condemned by the Labour leadership. The normally mild-mannered Donald Dewar, the shadow Scottish Secretary, said Galloway's actions amounted to collaboration.

Labour and the Liberal Democrats were in headlong retreat from the constitutional issue. As they tried to rally themselves, there was a conscious attempt to address real issues like education, employment and health, instead of the chattering class issue of home rule. It was only at the end of election year that interest began to be rekindled, when 25,000 people took to the streets of Edinburgh during the December summit of European Community leaders. When the marchers rallied in the Meadows afterwards, a Democracy Declaration was read out, concluding with the words:

'When the eyes of the world are on our capital, Edinburgh, we are confident that the peoples and governments of Europe will recognise the appeal of its host nation. We therefore raise our demand without fear or favour. Scotland demands democracy.'

For many who took part or read about it in the press, that show of strength in the Meadows lifted Scotland's general election hangover. But Labour remained reluctant to stoke up the home rule fires once again. In the absence of a renewed push on the constitution, opposition politics seemed lacklustre. Attacks were made on the run-down of the Rosyth naval base, the attempted gerrymandering of local government and the removal of water from local democratic control. But the opposition parties' hearts did not seem in it. The next general election looked an awful long way away. Opposition politics was a dour, almost ritualistic carping at the actions of a complacent Scottish Office.

The first Scotland United rally in Glasgow's George Square. The protest groups that sprang up after the 1992 election demonstrated the frustration many Scots felt at the result, but most failed to find a meaningful role.

So when a Liberal Democrat councillor in Strathclyde suggested a region-wide referendum on the water issue there was a weary and cynical reaction by some senior Labour politicans. They doubted its chances of success and some even felt it could prove an embarrassment.

When the results came through the outcome was unambiguous: 97% of those who took up the offer of a postal ballot voted against the government's plans. The remarkable thing was the turnout. Well over a million people, an incredible 71.5% of those eligible to vote, took part. For a postal ballot, this was extraordinary. It was an overwhelming rejection of a particularly insensitive Tory policy. But it had a additional significance. The message from Strathclyde was that Scots did not want less democratic control over their own affairs, they wanted more. The democratic deficit that allowed the Tories to impose their water policy on unwilling Scots was thrown into stark relief.

The Scottish Office was startled; it had not counted on a popular uprising.

People power, as expressed in the Strathclyde water referendum, invigorated opposition politics.

117

Caught off-guard, minister Allan Stewart was bullish and dismissive, striking a discordant note. Somewhat chastened, Labour politicians made public their admiration for those who had taken part. People power had brought a sense of outrage back into Scottish politics in general and the home rule cause in particular.

Labour Pains

In the contest to replace Neil Kinnock as Labour leader, the runaway victor was John Smith, an Edinburgh advocate whose bank manager appearance was immediately reassuring to would-be voters. Labour's home rule enthusiasts, who had always been suspicious of Kinnock because of his 1970s opposition to devolution, were also more at ease. As a young minister in the Callaghan government, Smith had been in charge of detailing the devolution legislation, and the failure to achieve an assembly in 1979 had always irked him. Devolution was the settled will of the Scottish people, he said, and Labour could be counted on to deliver this time. Tragically, he was to be denied the chance to complete what he called his unfinished business.

On the morning of 12 May 1994, John Smith suffered a heart attack at his London flat in the Barbican and died. He was 55. Across Britain the sense of loss was profound. The funeral in his local church in Edinburgh's Morningside took on the character of a state occasion, with mourners from all over the world. Despite being leader for only 22 months, he had achieved much, restoring the party's credibility after the 1992 defeat, and carrying on the process of Labour's modernisation through the introduction of one-member one-vote in key areas of party democracy. Above all, he had made Labour believe again that it could win back power.

The Monklands East by-election caused by Smith's death was a reminder of some of the harsh truths about urban Scotland. Sectarianism was rife. Areas of the constituency that were predominantly Protestant were resentful at what they saw as the bias exercised by the overwhelmingly Catholic Labour council, which was allegedly pouring cash into projects in Catholic districts. A poll showed 85% of Catholics intended to vote Labour and 65% of Protestants intended to back the Nationalists. Many party campaigners and spindoctors parachuted in for the contest were completely unprepared for this strain of politics. To enormous Labour relief, its candidate, Helen Liddell, scraped home with a majority of 1,640, a tenth of that enjoyed by Smith. Although the result was embarrassing for Labour in such an area and under such circumstances, it was hard to see this as a moral victory for the Nationalist cause. It was more a salutary reminder of one of the darker sides of the Scottish psyche.

John Smith died of a heart attack on 12 May 1994. He was buried on the island of Iona, near a burial mound believed to be the resting place of ancient Scottish kings.

A shocked Ian Lang struggles to fight back tears as he holds an impromptu press conference at the Scottish Conservative conference in Inverness on hearing of the death of John Smith.

The battle for Smith's old seat, Monklands East, was fought in an atmosphere of tense sectarian bigotry, and almost delivered the SNP an historic win. But Labour's Helen Liddell fought off the challenge to claim a narrow victory.

One post-election protest group that did have a degree of staying power was Democracy for Scotland, which staged a long-running vigil outside the parliament building on Edinburgh's Calton Hill.

The contest had a more disturbing message for the Scottish Labour leadership. It was that misdemeanours, real or imagined, of Labour fiefdoms in local government could be used effectively against the party in other elections. Criticism was being levelled at other Labour councils – in Dumbarton, Renfrew, Dundee, Motherwell, Aberdeen – the list went on. The Labour criticism of the Tory government as venal and lazy after so long in power seemed equally applicable to Labour's local heartlands. Labour strategists knew there was little point in projecting the party as a bright new alternative government when the voter saw Labour locally as complacent and possibly corrupt. It was getting harder to counter those critics of devolution who asked if people really wanted a Scottish parliament full of former Labour councillors who fancied a change of scenery and a fat salary.

Many home rule enthusiasts wanted to see Gordon Brown replace Smith as

121

Cometh the hour: After Smith's death, Tony Blair sidelined his close ally Gordon Brown to clinch the Labour leadership.

Labour leader. They believed he would ensure the party stuck to the commitment on a Scottish parliament that Smith held so dear. But it was Tony Blair, a Scots-born barrister educated at Fettes public school in Edinburgh, who was to sideline Brown and clinch the prize. Blair, the youngest-ever Labour leader, was an instant hit with traditional Tory supporters in much of the London-based press. But would Scotland take to this public schoolboy? There were concerns in Scottish Labour about early private polling evidence suggesting he might be a turn-off for Scottish voters. But Blair proved to be a tonic for Scottish Labour, taking the party to over 50% in the opinion polls.

It did not take long for 'Bambi' Blair to bare his teeth. He embarked on a review of Labour policy that was breathtaking in its ruthlessness. The cherished Clause Four of the party's constitution, committing Labour to public ownership for the public good, was the most notable victim. The home rule plans approaching completion in the Scottish Constitutional Convention after six years of haggling came under the same scrutiny. Out went the agreed scheme for funding the parliament, the proposal for keeping Scottish income tax and VAT returns in Scotland. Out went Labour's apparent acceptance of a parliament of around 150 members. And out went the plan for regional assemblies across England to spread devolution south of the border, which the Labour leadership had previously boasted would finally provide a riposte to Tam Dalyell's West Lothian question. Opposition to these changes was muted. Activists were constantly being reminded that the general election was not won yet, and few wanted to be seen to launch a full-blooded attack on a leader who was the party's best hope of power for a generation.

The only voice that refused to be silenced was Tam Dalyell's. Risking the wrath of the Blair camp, the Linlithgow MP again raised his infamous West Lothian question and went public with his view that there should be another Scottish referendum on devolution. The leadership ridiculed him, saying he was in a minority of one. There was no need, they insisted, for a referendum. A general election victory would be mandate enough for devolution.

Salmond's Stepping Stone

Alex Salmond made himself a promise in the aftermath of the 1992 general election. Never again would the SNP put so much into a campaign and come out with so little. Next time, if the party was not going to win independence, it would make sure it at least came out of the contest stronger. It had been called the 'independence election' by some Nationalists, and the SNP seemed on a roll. The Scottish edition of the *Sun*, locked in a bitter and highly personalised circulation

Alex Salmond brought a new professionalism and level-headedness to SNP politics. But his gradualist views put him at odds with some of his more fundamentalist colleagues.

war with the Labour-supporting *Daily Record*, came out in favour of Scottish independence. According to one account, editor Bob Bird arranged for a piper to gatecrash a News International management meeting in London before he pitched the idea to a bemused Rupert Murdoch. 'Rise Now and Be a Nation Again', was the tabloid's message. Culled from the folk song *Flower of Scotland*, it became a car sticker and soon became a familar sight on Scotland's roads, albeit that many motorists cut off the *Sun* logo first.

Under the influence of charismatic deputy leader Jim Sillars, the SNP had adopted an uncompromising all-or-nothing strategy, claiming Scotland was on the very brink of becoming a sovereign state once more. 'Free By 93', was the slogan created by Sillars's lieutenant Alex Neil. It was a phrase designed to give Scots confidence that independence was within reach; all that was needed was one final heave.

In the end, voters stuck with the unionist devils they knew, and the surge failed to materialise. It was too much for Sillars, who on losing his Govan seat bowed out of active politics to concentrate on business interests and to snipe at Salmond in a *Sun* column. The Scots, he said, were '90-minute patriots', who lacked the bottle to go it alone. Free of his main rival for the party's affections and loyalty, Salmond was now very much in charge. A gradualist by instinct and inclination, he publicly acknowledged the 'Free by 93' fundamentalist approach was a mistake. It was not one he had any intention of repeating.

Despite the election result, the notion of independence had become more credible than at any time in the SNP's past. At the height of the party's electoral success in the 1970s, the party's popularity far outstripped backing for independence as an idea. By the 1990s that was reversed. Supporters of independence varied between a quarter and half of all Scots, well ahead of the SNP's own support. This was allied to a shift in people's attitude to their national identity. Polls showed that Scots who felt predominantly British were outnumbered more than 2-1 by those who felt mostly Scottish; less than one in ten felt just British.

Cultural nationalism, albeit with a small 'n', was on the rise. A generation of young Scots had never heard of 'the Scottish cringe', and found it difficult to comprehend when explained to them. Scotland had its own cultural hinterland beyond the tartanry of Hogmanay celebrations and the couthiness of the *Sunday Post*. Rock bands such as Deacon Blue, The Proclaimers and Runrig explored their Scottishness in their music to international as well as domestic acclaim. The same was true in Scottish literature, with the international success of novelists Jim Kelman, Alasdair Gray and Iain Banks, later to be joined in spectacular fashion by Irvine Welsh. The paintings of Glasgow artists Peter Howson, Steven Conroy and Steven Campbell were hung on the walls of some of the richest and most famous people in the world. Scots were less apologetic about their Scottishness, more sure of it and at ease with it, than ever before.

Acts such as Runrig played a key role in the Scottish cultural renaissance in the 1980s and 1990s. They played Celtic rock music firmly based in the Scottish experience and Scottish traditions, and sold records worldwide.

The independence movement's growing credibility was enhanced by the Scots' affinity for Europe. The SNP's policy of Independence in Europe, adopted in 1988, showed the party in its best light, outward-looking, modern and internationalist, as opposed to the insular, inward-looking sect it had sometimes appeared in the past. European parliament elections in 1994 produced the SNP's best share of the vote since the 1970s – 33% – and gave the party two out of Scotland's eight MEPs. There was talk of a 'seismic change' in Scottish politics.

Like so many other SNP surges since the war, however, this one proved unsustainable. The reason was the growing strength of the Labour Party. The SNP mantra 'Labour can't win' was designed to attract those voters who had stuck with Labour through thick and thin, but had tired of waiting for the breakthrough. The slogan was used in contest after contest and became an article of faith for many Nationalists. But a nagging worry grew in the minds of SNP strategists – what if Labour could win? What then for the Nationalist cause?

Salmond firmly believed the best chance for the SNP's fortunes would come when Labour was in power and making unpopular decisions. That was the time to turn the heads of the massed ranks of Labour voters towards the bright future offered by the Nationalists. And crucially, although it was difficult for him to say this publicly, he also thought the most realistic way of achieving independence was by using a devolved parliament as a springboard, or stepping stone. This was anathema to the fundamentalist wing of his party. For them, devolution was the enemy.

When *Scotland on Sunday* published a front-page story in January 1995 with the headline 'Salmond backs devolution', the SNP leader was able to make good use of the resulting furore to edge his party away from a fundamentalist approach. Salmond had told the paper the party should not get 'hung up on the route' Scotland took to independence. Getting there by means of devolution was equally valid as getting there by winning a majority of Scottish seats in a UK general election; the latter was not a 'holy grail'. The fundamentalist wing was predictably outraged. Devolution, they argued, was a dead end for Scotland. It could delay independence for 'hundreds of years', according to one national executive member. Salmond made the row an issue of confidence in his leadership. He knew he would win backing of the party's executive for his approach, but his winning margin of 17-6 showed a substantial section of the party still opposed his strategy. He described it, somewhat ambiguously, as a 'fairly resounding endorsement'.

The SNP would head for the general election campaigning on a platform of independence, and it remained the SNP's primary aim. But unlike in 1992 there would be no attempt to march the Scottish nation up to the top of the freedom hill only to have it march right down again. The party would portray itself as the guarantor of a devolved parliament, and as the 'power for change' in Scottish politics. Pragmatism, patience and level-headedness – never the strongest Nationalist virtues, would be the keys to future success.

Forsyth's New Unionism

Every government has to put up with being unpopular. But none in living memory had sunk as low in public esteem as John Major's administration by the mid-1990s. Conservative fortunes had been in the doldrums since Black Wednesday – 16 September 1992 – when Britain retreated unceremoniously from the European exchange rate mechanism and confidence in Major's government slumped.

Magnified by the harsh scrutiny of a previously loyal press, disillusionment with the Tories' perceived abuse of power dominated political life. Sleaze, a catch-all description for every kind of moral and ethical lapse, seemed to permeate every pore of his administration. The 'back-to-basics' strategy on traditional values was regarded as a licence to reveal the peccadillos of MPs' private lives, and at one stage the resignation of ministers seemed a weekly occurrence. The arms-to-Iraq affair revealed duplicity and subterfuge as commonplaces of government, with ministers and civil servants strangely unable to discern the definition of 'truth'. And when Tory MPs were revealed as willing to accept four-figure sums to place parliamentary questions, it seemed the popular perception was true – politicians had a price.

In Scotland the Tories hit rock bottom. In the 1995 elections to the new single-tier local authorities the party could manage only 11% of the vote. Conservatives failed to win control of a single Scottish council. Scottish politics seemed like a straight fight between the SNP and Labour, a perception underlined by the Great Debate between Salmond and Labour's George Robertson in the putative parliament building in Edinburgh. The event introduced 'the Lorraine Mann question' to the political lexicon, with Robertson unable to say what his second-best constitutional option would be.

Despite the fact that Scots were enjoying the benefits of a buoyant Scottish economy, the Tories still took the flak. Since February 1992, Scottish unemployment had been lower than the UK rate for the first time in living memory. Partly, this was due to a string of inward investment successes. But the main explanation was that Scotland had suffered less than England in the recession, and having gone into it late had been able to recover more quickly. Tory strategists were dismayed that this relative prosperity was not being translated into grateful backing for the government.

Discontent in Tory ranks was beginning to be aimed at Ian Lang, whose patrician style was regarded by some as a liability. When a beleaguered Major

On his return to Scotland, Michael Forsyth was compared by one tabloid newspaper to the horror film monster Freddie Kreuger. But he immediately tried to belie his image by striking a consensual note.

decided he needed his friend and ally in a more senior Cabinet position there was only one realistic replacement in the Scottish Office. Michael Forsyth was the only Scottish Tory of a high enough calibre. When his return was first mooted, many Tories rejected the notion as outrageous and impossible. In his previous spell as junior Scottish Office minister he antagonised Scotland's teachers and enthusiastically administered the Thatcherite medicine with little concern for how it tasted. In his time as Scottish party chairman, he reduced the Scottish Tories to a state of civil war. Forsyth was undoubtedly the least popular politician in Scotland, a hate figure who personified for many the Thatcherite disregard for Scottish sensibilities and interests.

A period of exile as a junior minister in the Home Office had, however, given him time to reflect, and to hone and smooth his political style. When he returned as Scottish Secretary he was at first almost unrecognisable in his approach. Consensual in tone, he was apparently willing to listen and respond to diverse points of view. At best, Forsyth would have less than two years to make his mark and rescue the fortunes of the Tories, languishing in the low teens in the Scottish opinion polls. It soon became clear there was one central theme in his strategy – he was going to put the Scottish back into the Scottish Conservative and Unionist Party.

On the doorsteps in successive election campaigns in Scotland, Tory canvassers had come up against the same sentiment – the party was seen as English-dominated, even anti-Scottish. Lang, who often came across as distant and aloof, had been determined not to play the Scottish card too readily. He feared it would undermine the sense of British pride and faith in the Union he was trying to encourage. As for considering devolution, why be the least enthusiastic of four parties advocating some kind of home rule? Lang's instinct was to sit tight, warn darkly of the break-up of the UK, and hope yet another rallying call to the defence of the Union at the next election, coupled with a tax cut, could result in the Tories holding on.

Forsyth had other ideas. From his first day in the Scottish Office, he acted as if he was a card-sharp with a pack full of Scottish aces. Every opportunity to fight Scotland's corner or take a lead on the domestic issue of the moment was leapt upon – saving the threatened sleeper service to Fort William, giving government-owned crofts back to crofters, boosting the Scottish film industry, banning a widely abused form of temazepam and launching an all-party crusade against drugs. Forsyth presented himself as a battler in Whitehall for Scottish interests. The Tories' Scottish conference in spring 1996 introduced a new party slogan, 'Fighting for Scotland', and new logo featuring a lion rampant. It was not putting a kilt on the party, as some cynics claimed. It was more a case of allowing a party that had seen its Scottish identity eroded over the past three decades to get its kilt out of mothballs.

But there was a line that Forsyth would not cross. There would be no elected Scottish parliament to take control of Scottish affairs. Westminster had to remain sovereign. Anything else would lead inevitably, he said, to the break-up of Britain. Instead Forsyth introduced yet more reforms of parliamentary process, including the introduction of a 'grand tour' of the Scottish Grand Committee around Scottish cities. Through the setting up of advisory bodies like the revamped Scottish Economic Council he tried to give Scottish pressure groups a greater say in government affairs. But the bottom line was no direct democratic control. Forsyth nevertheless displayed his chutzpah by declaring his strategy for Scotland amounted to real devolution, unashamedly appropriating the d-word. Would it be enough? It was, he said, his 'best shot'.

Labour was wrong-footed, unsure whether to tease Forsyth for his hypocrisy or try to take credit for forcing a change of mind. But this dilemma was nothing compared to the trauma about to be inflicted on Labour by Forsyth's secret weapon – the tartan tax.

The phrase was actually coined by Lang, but Forsyth made it his own. The tartan tax was the revenue-raising power proposed in the Constitutional

The tartan tax was Forsyth's masterstroke, accurately aimed at the Labour Party's weakest flank. It produced near-panic in Labour ranks and a dramatic U-turn.

The Constitutional Convention launched its blueprint for a Scottish parliament on St Andrew's Day 1995. The document ducked some major issues and fudged others, but succeeded in creating an agreed plan for moderate home rule that enjoyed wide acceptance. Its proponents said it heralded a new style of politics. Labour and the Liberal Democrats agreed that half their candidates would be women.

Convention's plan for a Scottish parliament. A Scottish government would have the power to vary the basic rate of income tax by up to 3p in the pound. It was obvious to Forsyth that this was Labour's weakest flank, and one easily assailed. He simply pointed out with relentless regularity that if the tax was levied, Scots would end up with lighter paypackets than people in England doing the same job and earning the same wage. It would, he said, be a tax on being Scottish.

For a Labour Party still smarting at the damage the tax issue inflicted in the 1992 general election, this was the sorest of sore points. Despite all the work done in persuading the British electorate that new Labour was no longer the tax-and-spend party of old, the Tories could now say Blair was intent on imposing a new income tax on millions of Britons. Labour's George Robertson tried to brazen it out, insisting the tartan tax was just a power, and one he would be extremely unlikely to use. But this argument carried little weight in the face of Forsyth's onslaught.

In the spring of 1996, with Labour demoralised at being pinned down over the tartan tax, opposition politics in Scotland was again in the doldrums. And again it took a show of people power to invigorate the political debate, just as the Strathclyde water referendum had done two years before. A march in Edinburgh of parents, teachers and children protesting at education cuts attracted an extraordinary 40,000 people. The figure was a police estimate – usually a conservative one. It was the biggest political rally in Scotland since the Upper Clyde Shipbuilders marches in the 1970s. It gave the lie to the cynical assumption of politicians and commentators that protest was dead.

The education rebellion confirmed Forsyth could not escape the consequences of public spending cuts ordered by the Cabinet of which he was a member. It was going to be more difficult than he thought to distance himself from the unpopularity of the British Tory government. Worryingly for him, his bravura performance as Scottish Secretary was proving slow to translate into increased support in the opinion polls. The only consolation was the enduring belief that pollsters consistently underestimated the Tory vote. Privately, some Tories began thinking of the opportunities a Scottish parliament would give them to create a distinctly Scottish Conservative party free of the taint of its London leadership.

In the long run-up to his second general election as party leader, John Major ensured Scottish home rule would be central to the campaign. Defending the Union had paid off for him in 1992, and perhaps it could do so again. With Blair's new Labour Party increasingly indistinguishable from the Tories on a number of policy fronts, it was the constitution that provided the clearest blue water between the two main UK parties.

Happily for Major, defending the Union from devolution chimed with his main political preoccupation: Europe. Tory strategists saw a benefit in portraying Major as a defender of Britain on two fronts, against those who would break it into pieces through devolution and those who would submerge its sovereignty in a European superstate.

Europe had been Thatcher's downfall and it threatened to be Major's as well. It was constant pressure from his Eurosceptic wing that led to his surprise resignation as party leader and his successful re-election in July 1995, albeit without the backing of a third of his MPs. By adopting a harder line on Europe and playing down Britain's likelihood of joining a single European currency, he was able to shore up his backbench support. But Europe was a constant threat. As one of those backbenchers commented, it was unclear from a distance whether he was leading the Eurosceptics or being chased by them.

While it was the British flag Major was waving, it was mainly little England's attention he wanted to attract. A fledgling English nationalism could be detected in the country. It could be seen in the St George's flags, not Union flags, being waved in the Euro 96 football tournament, and in endless musings on the nature of Englishness in the London-based quality press.

Labour seemed unsure how to deal with this twin upsurge of English nationalism and Euroscepticism, but it was fertile ground for Major's brand of patriotic Toryism. Central Office campaigners were keen to cultivate it, even if it meant

The Scottish heavyweights in Labour's shadow Cabinet came north to announce a new policy on devolution. Scots were to be asked to vote in a referendum despite the fact that this tactic had been ruled out by the labour leadership a number of times in the past. (Left to right) Robin Cook, Jack McConnell (Scottish Labour Party General Secretary), Donald Dewar, George Robertson, Gordon Brown.

alienating some continental Europeans and Scots in the process. In his attempt to interest English voters in the constitutional agenda Major depicted the Scots as dangerous wreckers. Devolution – which had been official Tory policy 20 years before – was now 'teenage madness'. The Scots were wrong, and the Tories knew better.

Major, however, was leaving himself open to the charge of inconsistency. While condemning devolution for Scotland, his administration was busy trying to create a devolved system of government for Northern Ireland. Tory ministers had always dismissed attempts to draw comparisons between devolution for Northern Ireland and devolution for Scotland. But it was beginning to look like an anomaly.

With a Labour victory likely, and anticipation of a Scottish parliament rising, Labour anxieties about its tax-raising powers became increasingly plain. Forsyth's tartan tax campaign demanded a response, but the Labour leadership's chosen riposte took Scotland completely by surprise and threw the home rule debate into turmoil. Amid an orgy of speculation, the Scottish heavyweights in Blair's shadow Cabinet came north in June 1996 to announce a general election victory

George Robertson and Tony Blair during the Labour leader's mission to Scotland to explain the need for a referendum. It was to be the first of three U-turns, provoking a crisis of confidence in Labour's devolution plans.

"Tony doesn't give a ✖✖ for a Scottish Parliament"

For the SNP, the referendum U-turn was proof that 'You can't trust Labour.'

A SCOTTISH PARLIAMENT

IT'S A GAMBLE WITH THE SNP

Scottish Labour

Labour took advantage of the SNP leadership's refusal to say which way they would urge their supporters to vote in a referendum

was no longer mandate enough for devolution. Before Scotland could have its parliament it would have to hold a referendum – the very policy they had ridiculed Tam Dalyell for advocating the previous year. The ghost of 1979 had come back to haunt Scottish politics.

It should have been a field day for the SNP, but the Nationalist reaction was mixed. Labour's 'betrayal' was presented as definitive proof that Blair could not be trusted. But Salmond was aware of the divisions another referendum could cause in his own ranks, and said he would not be drawn on his referendum stance before the general election.

Labour's partners in the Constitutional Convention expressed their outrage at the U-turn, but most were prepared, reluctantly, to go along with a referendum. What rankled was Labour's decision to pose two questions, one on the principle of a parliament itself and another on whether it should have tax powers. George Robertson claimed authorship of the tactical shift, but most observers saw the hands of Blair and shadow Chancellor Gordon Brown. Some suspected the leadership of trying to ditch the tax plans by proxy, an allegation strenuously denied by the leadership. Critics argued the second question made the tax powers seem like an optional extra, and not integral to establishing the parliament's autonomy and accountability as most constitutional experts believed.

Home rule enthusiasts in the Labour Party were furious and decided to campaign for the scrapping of the second question. The leadership was just as determined to keep it, not least because Blair had given it his public backing. At a

137

meeting of the party's Scottish executive on 31 August, the only way the leadership could avoid defeat was to accept a clumsy compromise involving three questions spread over two referendums. One bemused observer commented: 'Only in the Labour Party could a meeting to choose between a one-question referendum and a two-question referendum come up with a three-question referendum.'

It was an untenable position, and six days later Robertson threw it overboard, reverting to the two-question proposal. Labour had changed its mind three times in four months – not for the first time, its credibility on devolution had taken a hefty dent. The SNP and the Tories took great pleasure in their opponent's discomfort.

Before Labour's decision to hold a referendum there had been an unmistakable sense that Scotland was in the ante-room of history. Now two new locks had been put on the connecting door. A new nervousness struck the home rule camp. If the referendum went ahead it would be an epoch-making test of national confidence and self-belief. When it came down to it, did Scots really want home rule? And if so, how much power were they really willing to give their parliament? After 50 years of constitutional restlessness, the Scottish nation had an unrivalled opportunity to take a long hard look at itself, and decide its future.